The CIVIL WAR

R.G.W.
2019 — HANSON

Publications International, Ltd.

Writer: Martin F. Graham is the coauthor of several Civil War books including *The Civil War Chronicle, The Blue & the Gray, The Civil War Wall Chart, Great Battles of the Civil War,* and *Mine Run: A Campaign of Lost Opportunities.* He specializes in Civil War and World War II history and has contributed to *Civil War Quarterly, Civil War Times Illustrated,* and *Blue & Gray Magazine.* He has served as president of the Cleveland Civil War Round Table.

Contributing writers:
Clint Johnson
Richard A. Sauers, Ph.D.
George Skoch

Louis Weber, CEO
Publications International, Ltd.
8140 Lehigh Avenue
Morton Grove, Illinois 60053

ISBN: 978-1-64030-340-9

Manufactured in China.

8 7 6 5 4 3 2 1

Contents

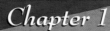
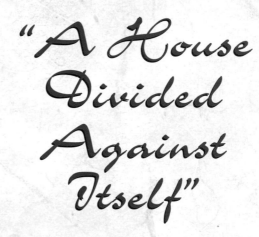

Chapter 1

"A House Divided Against Itself"

"A house divided against itself cannot stand. I believe this government cannot endure permanently half slave and half free."

—*Abraham Lincoln's Address to the Republican Convention, June 16, 1858*

"If the Northern states ... desire to inflict injury on us ... a terrible responsibility will rest upon it, and the suffering of millions will bear testimony to the folly and wickedness of our aggressors."

—*Confederate President Jefferson Davis's inaugural address*

James Massalon's painting captures the inauguration of Jefferson Davis as President of the Confederacy on February 18, 1861. The ceremony took place on the portico of the Alabama State House in Montgomery, which was then the Confederacy's capital city.

Jefferson Davis

"**The South** did not fall crushed by the mere weight of the North," observed Pierre G. T. Beauregard several years after the war, "but it **was nibbled away at all sides and ends because its executive head never gathered and wielded its great strength.**" Such was the feeling throughout much of the defeated South.

Davis was born on June 3, 1808, in Christian County, Kentucky. After graduation from West Point in 1828, he served in the army for seven years before retiring to a Mississippi plantation. His marriage to the daughter of future President Zachary Taylor lasted only three months before her death from malaria. He later married Varina Howell in 1845, the same year he was elected to Congress as a staunch advocate of states' rights.

He left Congress during the Mexican War and served as colonel of the 1st Mississippi Rifles. Wounded at the Battle of Buena Vista, he returned home a hero and was appointed by the Mississippi governor to fill a vacant seat in the Senate. His Senate career didn't last long, for he resigned in 1851 to make an unsuccessful run for governor. He returned to the national stage when President Franklin Pierce selected him to become secretary of war in 1853, a position he filled with distinction during a period of national and military expansion. He returned to the Senate in 1857 but resigned again four years later when Mississippi seceded from the Union. The Provisional Confederated Congress elected Davis provisional President on February 9, 1861, and he was formally elected President by popular vote on November 6, 1861.

Many felt Davis was a poor administrator as President, too involved in military concerns at the expense of civil affairs. As the fortunes of the Confederacy ebbed, those closest to Davis saw him gradually **change from a confident, poised leader to an inflexible chief executive, increasingly withdrawn** at a time when leadership and guidance were desperately needed.

Davis and his cabinet fled from Richmond prior to its fall in April 1865. He was finally captured on May 10 near Irwinville, Georgia, and imprisoned for two years before being released on bail. He spent several years traveling overseas before returning to Mississippi.

Davis died on December 9, 1889, without ever having his U.S. citizenship restored. He left an impact on American history, however; his obituary in *The New York World* stated, "A great soul has passed away." Congressional action in 1978 posthumously restored his citizenship.

"I can't spare this man," Lincoln said about **Ulysses Grant.** "He fights!"

"No terms except an unconditional and immediate surrender can be accepted."

—*Grant's terms for the surrender of Fort Donelson, Tennessee, on February 16, 1862, and the source of his nickname, Unconditional Surrender Grant*

Pierre Gustave Toutant Beauregard

With the war less than four months old, 43-year-old **Confederate General Pierre G. T. Beauregard**, of Louisiana Creole descent, had already experienced his second victory at the First Battle of Bull Run. His first military triumph occurred when he directed the bombardment that forced the surrender of Fort Sumter. Plagued by an inability to capitalize on his battlefield successes, however, Beauregard's victory at the **First Battle of Bull Run would prove to be the apex of his military career.**

The Firing on Fort Sumter

"The intelligence that Fort Sumter has surrendered to the Confederate forces ... sent a thrill of joy to the heart of every true friend of the South. The face of every southern man was brighter, his step lighter, and his bearing prouder than it had been before."

—*Editor of the* Montgomery Advertiser *on the fall of Fort Sumter*

Many Charleston residents reacted quickly to the first sound of cannon fire at Fort Sumter, South Carolina. Mary Chestnut wrote, "I put on my double-gown and a shawl and went to the house top. The shells were bursting toward the Fort. And who could tell what each volley accomplished of death and destruction."

Rear Admiral David G. Farragut is in the rigging of his ship, the USS *Hartford*, on August 5, 1864, during an extremely close-quarters battle with the CSS *Tennessee* in this painting by W. H. Overend. The *Hartford* went on to defeat the *Tennessee* and its fellow defenders of Mobile Bay, Alabama, shutting down one of the last outposts for Confederate blockade runners.

Steel mills produced the thousands of tons of steel needed to supply the Northern war effort with weapons and machinery. While a few large plants like this existed at the beginning of the war in Southern cities such as Chattanooga, Tennessee, and Richmond, Virginia, the resources necessary to produce quality steel were exhausted in the region by 1865.

Civil War Challenge

Place the following states in the order they seceded from the Union:

Alabama	Louisiana	Tennessee
Arkansas	Mississippi	Texas
Florida	North Carolina	Virginia
Georgia	South Carolina	

Civil War Challenge Answers

The Southern states seceded in the following order:

1. South Carolina
2. Mississippi
3. Florida
4. Alabama
5. Georgia
6. Louisiana
7. Texas
8. Virginia
9. Arkansas
10. Tennessee
11. North Carolina

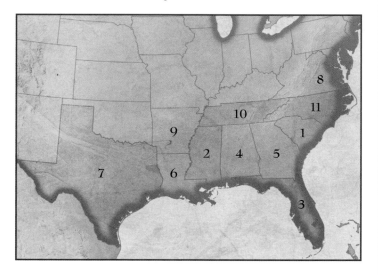

Missouri, Kentucky, Maryland, and Delaware were slave states that did not secede from the Union.

Suffering from dropsy, vertigo, and obesity, Winfield Scott was not up to the task of crushing the rebellion. However, the plan he devised before his retirement in 1861, calling for the blockade of Confederate ports and control of the Mississippi River, contributed to the Union victory.

"I implore gentlemen... whether from the South or the North... to pause at the edge of the precipice, before the fearful and dangerous leap be taken into the yawning abyss below, from which none who ever take it shall return in safety."

—Senator Henry Clay, February 5, 1850

As speaker of the House in 1820, Henry Clay crafted the Missouri Compromise, resolving the bitter conflict over the legality of slavery in territories from the Louisiana Purchase, which threatened to splinter the nation. Again, 30 years later, as senator from Kentucky, the 73-year-old Clay helped persuade Congress to settle its dispute over territories acquired after the Mexican War, earning him the title "The Great Pacificator."

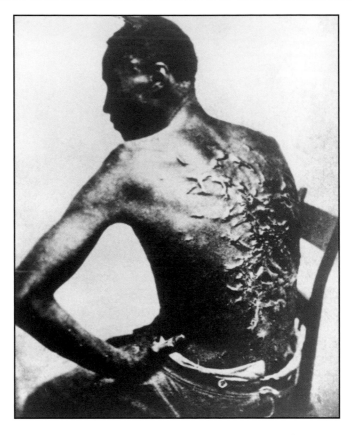

This escaped slave's bare back, scarred by lashes from a whip, shows the extent of plantation "justice" to a photographer in 1863. The master had complete power of discipline over his slaves.

Harriet Beecher Stowe

The appearance of *Uncle Tom's Cabin* in 1852 thrust Harriet Beecher Stowe into the middle of the slavery debate. Though of little literary merit, the novel's graphic portrayal of life on a Southern plantation appealed to those opposed to slavery, launching the book onto the best-seller lists throughout the North. Believing they had been unjustly stereotyped, citizens of the South united in their condemnation of the work.

First Battle of Bull Run

About three months after the surrender of Fort Sumter, 37,000 federal soldiers under General Irvin McDowell clashed with 35,000 Confederate troops commanded jointly by Generals P.G.T. Beauregard and Joseph E. Johnston near an obscure Virginia creek on July 21, 1861. **Ten hours of bitter fighting left 2,900 Union and 2,000 rebel casualties strewn on the battlefield** before McDowell's routed command fled back to the defenses of Washington. While the results of this battle **dashed the hopes of many Northerners** that the war would be brought to a swift conclusion, it **raised Southern hopes that they could win the conflict.**

Manassas National Battlefield Park

The first memorial at Manassas, Virginia, was a marker placed on the site where Colonel Francis Bartow, commander of a Confederate brigade, fell during the first battle there. The second memorial was a reddish-brown stone shaft erected by Union cavalry in the winter of 1864 near the site of heavy fighting adjacent to the Henry House. An inscription on the monument reads: "In memory of the Patriots who fell at Bull Run, July 21, 1861." It was later dedicated by a group of Union soldiers on July 21, 1865. About 128 acres on Henry Hill were purchased by the Sons of Confederate Veterans and the Manassas Battlefield Confederate Park, Inc., in 1922. The land was deeded to the National Park Service in 1938 as an "everlasting memorial to the soldiers of the Blue and Gray." The most popular monument in the park is the bronze equestrian statue of Stonewall Jackson erected on the alleged spot where the Confederate general received his nickname.

This 1860 carte de visite of **Abraham Lincoln** reveals something of the physical stature that earned him fame among his supporters and ridicule from his detractors. Not apparent, however, is his political stature, which achieved considerable heights throughout the North due to his position on slavery and his determination to keep the Union intact. **Lincoln's election as president in November 1860 proved to be the catalyst for the secession of Southern states.**

Meeting in Montgomery, Alabama, on February 4, 1861, delegates from seven Southern states elected **Jefferson Davis** President of the Confederate States of America. **The first and only Confederate chief executive,** shown here with his wife Varina, was determined to avoid hostilities with the federal government. But the unwavering desire of his people to break permanently from the Union doomed his country to war.

"Cotton is king and the African must be a slave, or there's an end of all things, and soon."

—Senator James Henry Hammond of South Carolina

The job of picking cotton in the field was rigorous for the unfortunate slave laborers. **Because cotton grew relatively low to the ground, overseers on horses could easily supervise the work.** The King Cotton economy ruled many of the Southern states before and after the war. This painting depicts plantation life along the Mississippi River. The cotton crop was planted in the spring, and harvesting and preparing the crop for sale normally extended into the early winter months.

The Southern Economy

The federal blockade of the Confederacy's coastline grew ever tighter as the war dragged on, and its increasing effectiveness had its greatest impact on the Confederate rate of inflation. In May 1861, a gold piece worth a dollar at U.S. rates was worth $1.10 in Confederate currency. By war's end, however, that same piece of gold was worth more than $60.00 in the Confederacy. This drawing shows the auction of a five-dollar gold piece in Virginia at the height of the money crisis.

"Dixie Land"

by Daniel Emmett

I wish I was in the land of cotton,
Old times there are not forgotten;
　　Look away! Look away!
　　　　Look away, Dixie Land!
In Dixie Land where I was born in,
Early on one frosty morning,
　　Look away! Look away!
　　　　Look away, Dixie Land!

(Chorus)
Then I wish I was in Dixie! Hooray!
　　Hooray!
In Dixie Land I'll take my stand, to
　　live and die in Dixie!
Away! Away! Away down South in
　　Dixie!
Away! Away! Away down South in
　　Dixie!

Old Missus married "Will the
　　Weaver";
William was a gay deceiver!
　　Look away! Look away!
　　　　Look away, Dixie Land!
But when he put his arm around
　　her,
Smiled as fierce as a forty-pounder!
　　Look away! Look away!
　　　　Look away, Dixie Land!

(Chorus)

His face was sharp as a butcher's
　　cleaver;
But that did not seem to grieve her!
　　Look away! Look away!
　　　　Look away, Dixie Land!

Old Missus acted the foolish part
And died for a man that broke
  her heart!
 Look away! Look away!
  Look away, Dixie Land!

(Chorus)

Now here's a health to the next
  old missus
And all the gals that want to
  kiss us!
 Look away! Look away! Look
  away, Dixie Land!
But if you want to drive away
  sorrow,
Come and hear this song
  tomorrow!
 Look away! Look away!
  Look away, Dixie Land!

(Chorus)

There's buckwheat cakes and
  Injun batter,
Makes you fat or a little fatter!
 Look away! Look away!
  Look away, Dixie Land!
Then hoe it down and scratch
  your gravel,
To Dixie's Land I'm bound to
  travel!
 Look away! Look away!
  Look away, Dixie Land!

(Chorus)

Top Civil War Reference Books

Title of Book	Author	# Volumes
War of the Rebellion: Official Records of the Union and Confederate Armies Important battle reports and communications of both Union and Confederate officers	U.S. War Dept.	128
A Compendium of the War of the Rebellion Regimental and battle statistics	Frederick H. Dyer	1
Regimental Losses in the American Civil War 1861–1865 Individual soldier, regimental, and battle statistics	William F. Fox	1
The Photographic History of the Civil War Thousands of photographs and descriptions	Francis T. Miller	10
Battles and Leaders of the Civil War Collection of post-war battle descriptions	Robert U. Johnson	4
Military Bibliography of the Civil War Important bibliography of Civil War books	C. E. Dornbusch	4
Lee's Lieutenants The perspective of leaders of the Confederate Army of Northern Virginia	Douglas S. Freeman	3
The Civil War Dictionary Descriptions of major Civil War features	Mark M. Boatner III	1
Historical Times Illustrated Encyclopedia of the Civil War Description of many diverse entries	Patricia L. Faust	1

A number of Civil War generals received their initial combat experience during the Mexican War of 1846–1848, including:

Winfield Scott
← Robert E. Lee
Ulysses S. Grant – – – →
Thomas J. "Stonewall" Jackson
George B. McClellan
Pierre G. T. Beauregard
Joseph E. Johnston

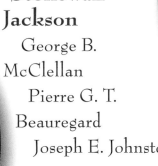

Colonel Jefferson Davis would become both the U.S. secretary of war and President of the Confederacy.

Women Spies

Throughout the war, **spies played an important role as a source of information for both sides.** Female agents were effective in using flattery and charm to entice information from enemy officers. The most famous of these included Pauline Cushman for the Union and Belle Boyd for the Confederacy.

Information from **Nancy Hart proved extremely helpful to Confederate commanders in western Virginia in 1862.** Captured by Union troops in July 1862, she escaped from her captors by taking a gun from her guard and shooting him dead. This photograph was taken the same day.

Rose O'Neal Greenhow was a well-established member of Washington society but used her connections to obtain confidential information that helped Confederate leaders prepare for the Union advance against Manassas in July 1861. Shown here with her daughter after she was captured and jailed, Greenhow later drowned when smuggling gold into the Confederacy amid heavy seas.

Sarah Emma Edmonds went undercover posing as both men and women to gather information to help the Union. One of her guises was as Union infantry soldier Frank Thompson. Her fellow troops never knew her secret until she showed up without the disguise at an 1884 reunion.

"That on the first day of January, in the year of our Lord one thousand eight hundred and sixty-three, all persons held as slaves within any State or designated part of a State, the people whereof shall then be in rebellion against the United States, shall be then, thenceforward, and forever free."

—*Abraham Lincoln's Emancipation Proclamation*

Lincoln presents his preliminary Emancipation Proclamation to his Cabinet.

Frederick Douglass

Frederick Augustus Washington Bailey was born a slave on February 7, 1817, in Tuckahoe, Maryland. His mother was black, and his father was a white master. Posing as a freed man, Bailey escaped north in 1838 and changed his last name to Douglass. He married Anna Murray and moved to Bedford, Massachusetts. Taught to read and write at an early age by the wife of a slaveholder, he became an eloquent spokesman for abolition.

"In thinking of America," Douglass wrote, "I sometimes find myself admiring her bright blue sky—her grand old woods. . . . But my rapture is soon checked when I remember that all is cursed with the infernal spirit of slaveholding and wrong; when I remember that with the waters of her noblest rivers, the tears of my brethren are borne to the ocean, disregarded and forgotten; that her most fertile fields drink daily of the warm blood of my outraged sisters, I am filled with unutterable loathing."

Douglass traveled to Europe, where he wrote his autobiography and raised $600 to purchase his freedom. Returning to the United States, he published a weekly abolitionist newspaper, *The North Star,* and assisted the federal government in raising black regiments throughout the war. He served as U.S. Minister to Haiti from 1889 to 1891 and died on February 20, 1895.

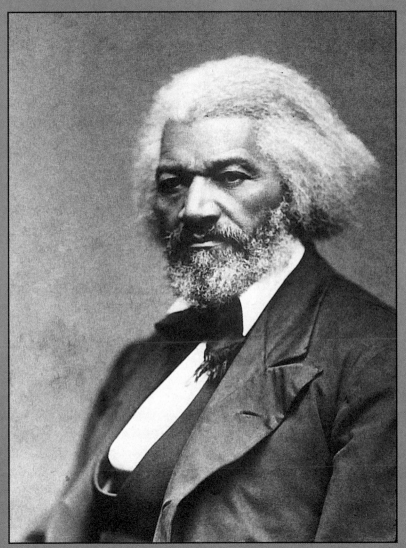

"On Wednesday evening we reached that historic village named Fairfax Court House. The inhabitants, what few there were, looked at us with astonishment, as if we were some great monsters risen up out of the ground. They looked bewildered, yet it seemed to be too true and apparent to them that they really beheld nearly 10,000 colored soldiers filing by, armed to the teeth, with bayonets bristling in the sun—and I tell you our boys seemed to fully appreciate the importance of marching through a secesh town. On, on we came, regiment after regiment, pouring in, as it seemed to their bewildered optics, by countless thousands—with colors flying and the bands playing; and, without intending any disparagement to other regiments, I must say the 43d looked truly grand, with the soldierly and imposing forms of our noble and generous Colonel and Adjutant C. Bryan riding at the head."

—*Sergeant John C. Brock, 43rd U.S. Colored Troops, describing the regiment's march to join the Army of the Potomac, May 1864*

Anxious to fight, black Union troops often found themselves relegated to guarding forts, camps, and prisoners. When they were allowed into battle, they were often thrown into wasted combat in engagements such as those at Fort Wagner, South Carolina, on July 18, 1863, and Olustee, Florida, on February 20, 1864.

Philip Sheridan

In his recommendation for Philip Sheridan's promotion to brigadier general of volunteers, Union General William Rosecrans wrote, "He is worth his weight in gold." Only five months earlier, the 31-year-old federal officer had been a commissary captain. On October 8, 1862, the conduct

of his division at the Battle of Perryville, Kentucky, drew praise from his superiors and marked the beginning of a meteoric rise unrivaled in the Union army during the course of the war.

Civil War Challenge

Match the battles with their dates:

Battle of Antietam/Sharpsburg	July 1–3, 1863
Battle of Five Forks	June 27, 1864
Battle of Shiloh/Pittsburg Landing	December 31, 1862 to January 2, 1863
Battle of First Bull Run/Manassas	September 17, 1862
Battle of Chickamauga	August 30, 1862
Battle of Gettysburg	December 13, 1862
Battle of Stones River/Murfreesboro	April 6–7, 1862
Battle of Fredericksburg	April 1, 1865
Battle of Kennesaw Mountain	July 21, 1861
Battle of Second Bull Run/Manassas	September 19–20, 1863

Civil War Challenge Answers

Battle of Antietam/Sharpsburg	September 17, 1862
Battle of Five Forks	April 1, 1865
Battle of Shiloh/Pittsburg Landing	April 6–7, 1862
Battle of First Bull Run/Manassas	July 21, 1861
Battle of Chickamauga	September 19–20, 1863
Battle of Gettysburg	July 1–3, 1863
Battle of Stones River/Murfreesboro	December 31, 1862 to January 2, 1863
Battle of Fredericksburg	December 13, 1862
Battle of Kennesaw Mountain	June 27, 1864
Battle of Second Bull Run/Manassas	August 30, 1862

Northern and Southern males, anxious to take part in the fighting before it ended, **flocked to recruiting stations** in the early months of the war. But their romantic visions of military life were quickly dispelled by the boredom and routine of the camps. Hours of drilling and idleness led these soldiers of both armies to yearn for the action of combat. Many would soon get their wish at the First Battle of Bull Run.

Chapter 2

"A Few Remarks"

"Government of the people, by the people, for the people, shall not perish from the earth."

—Abraham Lincoln, Gettysburg Address

Lincoln's Gettysburg Address

In early November 1863, President Abraham Lincoln received an invitation to "make a few remarks" at the dedication of the national cemetery at Gettysburg, Pennsylvania. The President accepted and arrived by train the night before the dedication.

After a long, slow procession to the cemetery south of the town, Edward Everett, a well-known orator, delivered an eloquent two-hour speech that ended in thundering applause. Lincoln then rose, stepped to the front of the platform, took out two sheets of paper, and delivered his two-minute tribute to the men who fought and died on that battlefield four months earlier.

"Fourscore and seven years ago our fathers brought forth on this continent a new nation, conceived in liberty, and dedicated to the proposition that all men are created equal.

"Now we are engaged in a great civil war, testing whether that nation, or any nation so conceived and so dedicated, can long endure. We are met on a great battlefield of that war. We have come to dedicate a portion of that field as a final resting-place for those who here gave their lives that this nation might live. It is altogether fitting and proper that we should do this.

"But, in a larger sense, we cannot dedicate—we cannot consecrate—we cannot hallow—this ground. The brave men, living and dead, who struggled here, have consecrated it far above our poor power to add or detract. The world will little note nor long remember what we say here, but it can never forget what they did here. It is for us, the living, rather, to be dedicated here to the unfinished work which they who fought here have thus far so nobly advanced. It is rather for us to be here dedicated to the great task remaining before us—that from these honored dead we take increased devotion to that cause for which they gave the last full measure of devotion; that we here highly resolve that these dead shall not have died in vain, that this nation, under God, shall have a new birth of freedom; and that government of the people, by the people, for the people, shall not perish from the earth."

Applause interrupted the speech five times, and a tremendous ovation and three cheers followed its completion. While Lincoln felt that his speech was a "flat failure," Everett summed up the impact of the President's "few words" when he wrote him the next day, "I should be glad, if I could flatter myself that I came as near to the central idea of the occasion, in two hours, as you did in two minutes."

Battle of Gettysburg

Considered by some as a turning point of the Civil War, the Battle of Gettysburg was fought from July 1 to July 3, 1863, in and around a small crossroads community in southern Pennsylvania. The battle marked the farthest point north reached by a Confederate army.

For three days, nearly 170,000 soldiers fought desperately against each other. The battle climaxed with Pickett's Charge, the final Confederate attempt to pierce the Union line. "In every direction among the bodies was the debris of battle," recalled a witness, "haversacks, canteens, hats, caps, . . . blankets, . . . bayonets, cartridge boxes. . . . Corpses strewed the ground at every step."

In May 1856, proslavery Missourians pillaged Lawrence, Kansas, a center of free-state sentiment in that region. A few days later, **fanatical abolitionist John Brown and several followers** avenged Lawrence by slaughtering five proslavers at Pottawatomie Creek, Kansas. This was only Brown's first step.

In 1859, he and his followers **seized the Federal arsenal in Harpers Ferry, Virginia,** seen below in 1865. **When Brown was executed later** that same year for his role in the raid, **the antislavery cause had gained its greatest martyr.**

"I, John Brown, am now certain that the crimes of this guilty land will never be purged away but with blood." 1859. —

— John Brown's note, passed to one of his guards on the gallows

The Battle of Antietam / Sharpsburg

On **September 17, 1862,** General Robert E. Lee's 40,000-strong Army of Northern Virginia collided with General George McClellan's Federal Army of the Potomac, numbering 75,000, along **Maryland's Antietam Creek. On the bloodiest day of the war, McClellan lost more than 12,500, while the Confederates suffered 13,700 casualties.** Although the result was a virtual stalemate, McClellan claimed victory when Lee's army fell back across the Potomac River into Virginia, ending the first rebel invasion of the North.

Antietam National Battlefield

The war was far from over when the Maryland state legislature dedicated a cemetery on the battlefield in March 1864 as "a proper burial place for the men who made the supreme sacrifice in the Maryland Campaign of 1862." Eleven acres were set aside for the graves of 4,776 Union dead. By the time the National Park Service took control of the battleground in 1933, there were 92 monuments on a 3,300-acre park. Much of the battlefield has been restored to its 1862 appearance, including the reconstruction of the Dunker Church. Of the 5,256 acres that presently make up the park, 840 are privately owned. Landmarks include:

Dunker Church

Bloody Lane /

    Sunken Road

Burnside Bridge

East and West Woods

Cornfield

National Cemetery

Dr. Mary Walker was a 28-year-old pioneering doctor when the war began. Signing up as a nurse, she eventually **worked her way up to assistant surgeon for an Ohio regiment,** insisting that her skills matched those of any male doctor. **Though never in combat, she successfully lobbied Congress for a Medal of Honor.** Because the Medal of Honor is intended to recognize valor in combat, Walker's

medal, along with 900 others, was revoked in 1917, but she refused to return it before her death in 1919. President Jimmy Carter reinstated her medal in 1977. Mary Walker is **the only woman to have received this most coveted military decoration.**

Dorothea Dix, known as a reformer for her activism on behalf of the mentally ill, became the Superintendent of Army Nurses during the Civil War.

Abraham Lincoln

"This morning, as for some days past," President Abraham Lincoln wrote on August 23, 1864, "it seems exceedingly probable that this Administration will not be re-elected. Then it will be my duty to so co-operate with the President elect, as to save the Union between the election and the inauguration; as he will have secured his election on such ground that he can not possibly save it afterwards." By the fall of 1864, the federal war effort was at perhaps its darkest moment as the November presidential election approached. But **the capture of Atlanta and victories in the Shenandoah Valley were the catalysts Lincoln needed to win the November election.**

Lincoln was born near Hodgenville, Kentucky, on February 12, 1809. He was primarily self-taught, and he received a license to practice law in 1836. Lincoln was elected to the U.S. House of Representatives in 1847 but lost a senatorial race in 1858. However, his performance in several debates with opponent Stephen A. Douglas drew national attention that helped launch Lincoln's successful bid for the presidency in 1860.

The strength of Lincoln's character and his resolve to save the Union has often been credited for holding the Federal

government together throughout its most difficult crisis. He was always affable and an excellent administrator. After several early mistakes, he turned military control over to the professionals while he paid closer attention to public matters. Although he found it personally painful to continue supporting the mounting cost of the war in human lives, his commitment to the vigorous prosecution of the war was ultimately rewarded with the defeat of the Confederacy.

Lincoln had little time to savor the reunification of the country, his goal for four years. On April 14, 1865, he was shot by John Wilkes Booth. His death the next morning sent shock waves throughout the North and South and marked the beginning of the long, difficult road to national reconciliation.

When observed from a distance, **these logs were effective as phony cannons that looked just as deadly as the real thing.** Johnny Reb and Billy Yank referred to them as **"Quaker guns."** In March 1862, Confederate forces left these "guns" in place when they abandoned their camps at Manassas. Union troops discovered the ruse when they occupied the site. "The rebels had mounted painted logs," observed a surprised bluecoat.

Civil War Challenge

Match the Union general with the battle he commanded:

George Meade	Antietam
Ulysses S. Grant	Corinth
George McClellan	Fredericksburg
Samuel Curtis	First Bull Run
William Rosecrans	Second Bull Run
Ambrose Burnside	Gettysburg
Joseph Hooker	Cedar Creek
Irvin McDowell	Vicksburg
John Pope	Pea Ridge
Philip Sheridan	Chancellorsville

Civil War Challenge Answers

George Meade	Gettysburg
Ulysses S. Grant	Vicksburg
George McClellan	Antietam
Samuel Curtis	Pea Ridge
William Rosecrans	Corinth
Ambrose Burnside	Fredericksburg
Joseph Hooker	Chancellorsville
Irvin McDowell	First Bull Run
John Pope	Second Bull Run
Philip Sheridan	Cedar Creek

These women are members of the **Soldiers Aid Society of Springfield, Illinois.** Desiring to make a difference while remaining on the home front, women such as these **banded together across the North to make or collect items of use for their loved ones in blue.** These supplies often included bandages, clothing, writing paper, pens, and food.

Harriet Tubman

One of the most famous and courageous conductors of the **Underground Railroad** was former slave Harriet Tubman. Following her own escape to freedom from a Maryland plantation in 1849, **she returned south 19 times to rescue more than 300 slaves, including her own family, from the "jaws of hell."**

Often called "Moses," since she led her people to the "Promised Land," Tubman recalled with pride that "my train never ran off the track and I never lost a passenger." During her sojourns south, she carried a gun to protect her group from slave catchers as well as to threaten those slaves who attempted to return to their plantations. "There was one or two things I had a right to, liberty or death," Tubman stated. "If I could not have one, I would have the other; for no man should take me alive; I should fight for my liberty as long as my strength lasted, and when the time came for me to go, the Lord would let them take me." **She was so infamous throughout the South that rewards for her capture once totaled more than $40,000.**

Tubman accompanied the Union Army to South Carolina, where she served as a nurse and scout. She lived among refugee blacks, helping them procure clothing, food, and shelter. **In June 1863, she went on a federal raid up the Combahee River to destroy railroad bridges and track down enemy troops. During this foray, she helped liberate about 750 slaves.**

Shiloh / Pittsburg Landing

Criticized for allowing the federal army into Tennessee following the loss of Fort Donelson, Confederate General Albert Johnston launched a surprise attack on April 6, 1862, against the command of General Ulysses S. Grant at Pittsburg Landing, Tennessee. Achieving initial success, Johnston's force of 40,000 was driven back the next day by Grant's reinforced troops, 62,000 strong. When the smoke cleared on this first major battle in the West, the rebels had been driven back to Corinth, Mississippi, leaving behind the body of their mortally wounded commander.

"I acted like a madman. . . . The feeling that was uppermost in my mind was to kill as many rebels as I could."

—Union soldier on experiencing combat

This 1880s lithograph shows "The Hornets' Nest" at Shiloh being defended by Union General Benjamin Prentiss, mounted on the horse on the right. It only hints at the savagery involved as the armies advanced and retreated, losing and regaining ground. Prentiss's division held this small section of the Sunken Road running through the woods for nearly six hours, enough time for U.S. Grant to form a final defensive line near the banks of the Tennessee River.

March 9, 1862, saw the first naval clash of ironclad vessels when the USS *Monitor* and the CSS *Virginia* (formerly the USS *Merrimack*) fought to a draw. Lieutenant John T. Wood of the *Virginia* described part of the battle.

"Several times the Monitor ceased firing, and we were in hopes she was disabled, but the revolution again of her turret and the heavy blows of her 11-inch shot on our sides soon undeceived us.

"Coming down from the spar-deck, and observing a division standing 'at ease,' Lieutenant Jones inquired:

"'Why are you not firing, Mr. Eggleston?'

"'Why, our powder is very precious,' replied the lieutenant; 'and after two hours' incessant firing I find that I can do her about as much damage by snapping my thumb at her every two minutes and a half.'"

Napoleonic Tactics

In the summer of 1856, U.S. Major Thomas J. Jackson fulfilled a lifelong dream. The man who would later earn fame as Stonewall Jackson in the Confederate Army toured Britain and much of Europe. He took special interest in the battleground of Waterloo. "His study of Napoleon and Wellington had been so thorough," one historian wrote, "that French officers with whom he conversed were often astonished."

Like many other ranking officers in the Union and Confederate armies, Jackson had been well versed in the tactics and feats of Napoleon Bonaparte. Napoleonic principles of rapid marches and maneuvers and the value

Napoleon Bonaparte

of exploiting geography dominated military education of the era. When the Civil War began, Union General in Chief Winfield Scott's strategy to defeat the South, nicknamed "The Anaconda Plan," adopted a classic Napoleonic concept: to surround, divide, and conquer an enemy. Some officers, such as Confederate General P.G.T. Beauregard and Union General George McClellan, even emulated Napoleon in posture and style, if not on the battlefield.

The end of the Civil War foreshadowed an end to Napoleonic tactics that called for bold frontal attacks by massed formations. Development of modern weapons, such as long-range rifled muskets and artillery, made such practices obsolete.

Fond of comparing himself to Napoleon, General George McClellan strikes a pose reminiscent of the French leader.

Lincoln's Secretary of War

Simon Cameron of Pennsylvania was Abraham Lincoln's first secretary of war. Cameron owed his appointment to his influential role in state politics and the fact that he "delivered" his state to Lincoln in the 1860 presidential election. Cameron's flagrant dispensation of patronage, as well as charges of corruption and general lack of experience, embarrassed Lincoln, who accepted Cameron's resignation in January 1862. The President then named Cameron the U.S. minister to Russia.

Lincoln chose **Edwin Stanton** as his next **secretary of war.** While Stanton made no secret of the fact that he **felt Lincoln was not suited to be president,** he competently ran the department for the remainder of the war. Stanton once remarked that Lincoln was "the original gorilla," but the President stood behind his secretary of war and admired his capacity for hard work. Stanton eventually came to admire Lincoln, but his earlier remarks seemed to be the basis for later groundless charges that he had a hand in Lincoln's assassination.

Judah P. Benjamin

A former U.S. senator, Judah P. Benjamin **served the Confederacy as attorney general, secretary of war, and secretary of state.** Born in the Virgin Islands in 1811, he was the product of Jewish parents from England. He entered Yale at age 14 but did not graduate. He later studied law with a firm in New Orleans and built a very successful practice of his own.

An eloquent orator, Benjamin was elected to the U.S. Senate in 1852, serving there until Louisiana seceded. Jefferson Davis named him the Confederacy's first attorney general, and from there he overcame anti-Semitism to become Davis's closest adviser. **Affable, with an affection for good living, Benjamin was referred to as "the Brains of the Confederacy."** After the war, he fled the country to become one of England's finest lawyers. He died in Paris in 1884.

With Atlanta in flames, William Tecumseh Sherman embarked on his march to the sea on November 15, 1864. Intent on destroying the Deep South's ability to wage war, his army cut a 60-mile-wide trail of wreckage through the heart of Georgia.

"I beg to present you as a Christmas gift the city of Savannah."

—*General William Sherman
to President Lincoln on December 22, 1864*

Gettysburg National Military Park

Shortly after the battle, David McConaughy, a Gettysburg lawyer, purchased parcels of land that played a major part in the battle, including tracts of Cemetery Hill, Little and Big Round Tops, and Culp's Hill. The Gettysburg Battlefield Memorial Association was formed in April 1864 to manage these sites and commemorate "the great deeds of valor... and the signal events which render these battlegrounds illustrious." About 600 acres were transferred to the federal government in 1895 and were established as the Gettysburg National Military Park. The land was turned over to the National Park Service in 1933. More than 1,400 monuments, tablets, and markers (many of them dedicated by veterans), as well as 300 cannons, and 90 period buildings cover the 5,907 acres, of which 1,854 are privately owned. Sites of particular interest include:

Eternal Light
Peace Memorial
High Water Mark

The Virginia Memorial
Gettysburg Cyclorama
National Cemetery

"With malice toward none;
with charity for all... to do
all which may achieve and
cherish a just and lasting
peace, among ourselves, and
with all nations."

—*Abraham Lincoln,*
second inaugural address, March 4, 1865

Lincoln delivered his second inaugural address from the portico of the Capitol. He is in the center behind the podium, reading from a sheet of paper he holds in both hands, pledging to prosecute the war to a successful conclusion.

George G. Meade

"I've been tried and convicted," George G. Meade stated upon assuming command of the Union Army of the Potomac, "and condemned without a hearing, and I suppose I shall have to go to execution." Three days later, Meade led his army into the greatest battle of the Civil War at Gettysburg,

Pennsylvania. Displaying sound generalship, he fought a solid defensive battle. His success would be tainted, however, when he was faulted for failing

to vigorously pursue the defeated Confederate army into Virginia.

Generals of the Union Army of the Potomac, shown here left to right, are Gouverneur Warren, William French, George Meade, Henry Hunt, Andrew Humphreys, and George Sykes.

Civil War Challenge

Match the Confederate general with the battle he commanded:

Nathan Bedford Forrest	Franklin
Braxton Bragg	Port Republic
Robert E. Lee	Cedar Creek
Earl Van Dorn	Shiloh
Joseph Johnston	Antietam
Ben McCulloch	Pea Ridge
Thomas "Stonewall" Jackson	Chattanooga
Jubal Early	Resaca
John Hood	Wilson's Creek
Albert Johnston	Fort Pillow

Civil War Challenge Answers

Nathan Bedford Forrest	Fort Pillow
Braxton Bragg	Chattanooga
Robert E. Lee	Antietam
Earl Van Dorn	Pea Ridge
Joseph Johnston	Resaca
Ben McCulloch	Wilson's Creek
Thomas "Stonewall" Jackson	Port Republic
Jubal Early	Cedar Creek
John Hood	Franklin
Albert Johnston	Shiloh

Abraham Lincoln named **Henry Halleck general in chief of all Union armies** as much for his reputation as a military genius as for his successes in the Western theater. **While he was a good administrator, he was not up to the task of designing and implementing a successful military strategy.** In March 1864 he was replaced by one-time subordinate Ulysses S. Grant.

Union soldiers surge into the Confederate defenses during the fighting at Cold Harbor, Virginia, on June 3, 1864. The 7th New York Heavy Artillery regiment seized rebel artillery and captured some prisoners, but a counterattack drove them back and restored the line. The 7th suffered 418 casualties at Cold Harbor, including the death of its colonel, Lewis Morris.

"The stench from the dead between our lines and theirs was sickening. It was so nauseating that it was almost unendurable; but we had the advantage, as the wind carried it away from us to them."

—*Federal soldier on the assault on Cold Harbor*

"Like a Stone Wall"

"Look, there stands Jackson like a stone wall. Rally behind the Virginians!"

—Confederate General Barnard Bee,
at the First Battle of Bull Run, July 1861

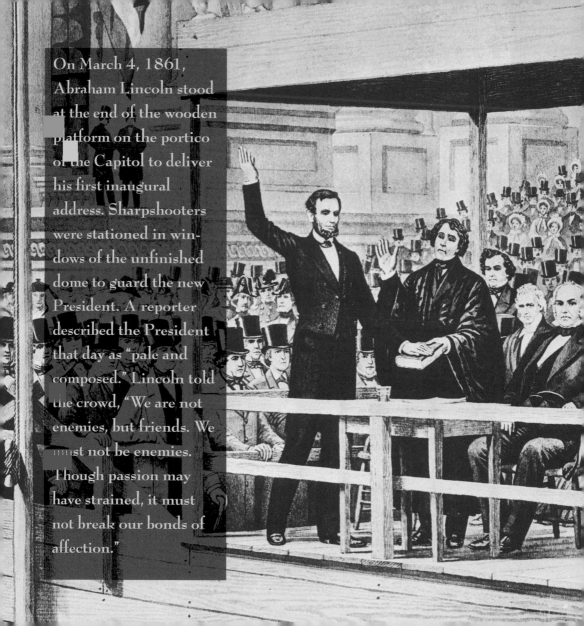

On March 4, 1861, Abraham Lincoln stood at the end of the wooden platform on the portico of the Capitol to deliver his first inaugural address. Sharpshooters were stationed in windows of the unfinished dome to guard the new President. A reporter described the President that day as "pale and composed." Lincoln told the crowd, "We are not enemies, but friends. We must not be enemies. Though passion may have strained, it must not break our bonds of affection."

Informed that **Robert E. Lee** had assumed command of the forces defending Richmond, General George McClellan stated, "I prefer Lee to [General Joseph E.] Johnston. The former is too cautious and weak under grave responsibility... wanting in moral firmness... likely to be timid and irresolute in action." Never had an assessment been so wrong on all counts. While confronting a larger, better-supplied force throughout his tenure as commander of the Army of Northern Virginia, Lee's **ability both to discover his enemy's weakness and to seize the initiative brought him success on many fields of battle.**

Robert E. Lee

"To save useless effusion of blood, I would recommend measures be taken for suspension of hostilities and the restoration of peace." This statement ended an appeal by General Robert E. Lee in early April 1865 to Confederate President Jefferson Davis to give up any idea of continuing hostilities through guerrilla-type warfare. Over the years, Lee has come to represent to many a model of honesty, integrity, and principle—a military genius whose campaigns are studied throughout the world.

The "Marble Man," a sobriquet given to Lee due to his larger-than-life stature, was born on January 19, 1807. His father, "Light Horse Harry" Lee, was a Revolutionary War hero and friend of George Washington. On June 30, 1831, Robert E. Lee solidified his standing in the Virginia aristocracy by marrying Mary Anne Randolph Custis, whose father was Washington's adopted son.

Lee graduated from West Point in 1829, second in his class. He served with distinction in the army for 32 years, including during the Mexican War. Union General Winfield Scott considered Lee "the very best soldier I ever saw in the field." Lee served as superintendent of West Point from 1852 to 1855. 3 yrs

He was on cavalry duty in Texas when Virginia seceded from the Union. Offered the command of the Union army by Scott, Lee declined. As with many officers with Southern roots, the decision to resign from the army was a difficult one for Lee. Even though he had taken an oath to defend the Union and was opposed to secession, Lee realized he could not take part in an invasion of Virginia or any other Southern state.

Throughout his command of the Confederate Army of Northern Virginia, he faced the unenviable challenge of confronting a far larger, better supplied force on battlefields in Virginia, Maryland, and Pennsylvania. His command eventually fell victim to the war of attrition waged by General Ulysses S. Grant. He

surrendered his beloved army at Appomattox Court House, Virginia, on April 9, 1865. He accepted the post of president of Washington College (since renamed Washington and Lee University) in September 1865, holding that position until his death on October 12, 1870. at 63 yrs of age.

CHARLESTON

MERCURY

EXTRA:

Passed unanimously at 1.15 o'clock, P. M., December 20th, 1860.

AN ORDINANCE

To dissolve the Union between the State of South Carolina and other States united with her under the compact entitled "The Constitution of the United States of America."

We, the People of the State of South Carolina, in Convention assembled, do declare and ordain, and it is hereby declared and ordained,

That the Ordinance adopted by us in Convention, on the twenty-third day of May, in the year of our Lord one thousand seven hundred and eighty-eight, whereby the Constitution of the United States of America was ratified, and also, all Acts and parts of Acts of the General Assembly of this State, ratifying amendments of the said Constitution, are hereby repealed; and that the union now subsisting between South Carolina and other States, under the name of "The United States of America," is hereby dissolved.

THE

UNION
IS
DISSOLVED!

By a vote of 169 to 0, the convention meeting in Charleston, South Carolina, voted to secede from the United States on December 20, 1860. "The cheers of the whole assembly continued for some minutes," wrote a delegate, "while every man waved or threw up his hat, and every lady waved her handkerchief." Six more Southern states followed South Carolina's lead by February 1, 1861.

As the **second session of the 37th federal Congress began in 1861**, the Democrats' Southern power base had disappeared, and the Republicans were well in control of both houses. The new majority party used their grip over Congress to pass legislation that changed the course of life in the United States. **The Internal Revenue, Pacific Railroad, and** Homestead acts were all results of the new vision brought to Congress by the Republican Party. **One of its most outspoken members was Pennsylvania Representative Thaddeus Stevens.**

Battle of Fort Donelson

After capturing Confederate Fort Henry on the east bank of the Tennessee River on February 6, 1862, General Ulysses S. Grant turned his attention to the other Confederate bastion, Fort Donelson, about 11 miles to the east on the west bank of the Cumberland River. For four days, under miserable winter conditions, Grant's 27,000 soldiers laid siege to the Confederate stronghold of 20,000 troops. After failing to break through federal lines, the Confederate commander, General Simon Buckner, wrote a note on February 16, 1862, to Grant, an old friend, requesting the "terms of capitulation of the force and fort." "Unconditional and immediate" was Grant's reply. White flags soon appeared above the rifle pits, and the surrender of this strategic Confederate fort followed.

On November 8, 1861, Confederate commissioners James M. Mason and John Slidell were on their way to Great Britain and France, respectively, in the hopes of bringing the European powers, who were starting to feel deprived of the Southern cotton they loved, into the conflict in support of the Confederacy. They had slipped through the Union blockade to Cuba and had boarded the British mail ship *Trent*, to sail from Havana to London. Roughly 300 miles east of Havana, however, they were intercepted by the Union warship *San Jacinto*, whose sailors boarded the *Trent*, seized the Confederates, and took them to jail in Boston. The British were furious that their ship, neutral in the War between the States, had been boarded and demanded the Confederate diplomats' release. Tensions grew between the countries, and for a time Great Britain appeared ready to declare its own war against the United States, with the possibility of France joining in, as well. *oh well!*

Lincoln realized that fighting two wars at once was more than the nation could manage, so he instructed Secretary of State William Seward to devise an acceptable resolution. Seward did just that by agreeing to release Mason and Slidell but refusing to admit guilt in the matter. The British were satisfied. The two Confederate commissioners did finally get to Europe, but their efforts to gain allies for the Confederacy ultimately came up dry.

Slaveholder Presidents

Slavery was so pervasive in American culture that it was taken as a matter of course that a man of wealth would own slaves. In fact, of the first dozen presidents, ten were or had been slave owners.

George Washington

Thomas Jefferson

James Madison

James Monroe

Andrew Jackson

Martin Van Buren

William Henry Harrison

John Tyler

James K. Polk

Zachary Taylor

The two early presidents who had never owned slaves were John Adams and his son, John Quincy Adams.

Civil War Challenge
Battle of Antietam

1. Whose corps began the attack at Antietam at about 5:30 A.M. on September 17, 1862?
2. What name was given to the sunken road in the middle of the Confederate position?
3. Whose Union corps was delayed in its attack on the rebel right flank because a little more than 500 Georgia and South Carolina troops blocked a bridge crossing Antietam Creek?
4. Two members of what federal regiment discovered Confederate General Robert E. Lee's Special Orders No. 191?
5. Whose corps arrived just in time to push back charging Union troops along the Confederate right flank?

Civil War Challenge Answers

1. General Joseph Hooker
2. Bloody Lane
3. General Ambrose Burnside
4. 27th Indiana Volunteer Infantry Regiment
5. General Ambrose Hill

Virginia native **Belle Boyd** took up spying for Stonewall Jackson in May 1862. She was captured, but Union General John A. Dix gave the young woman a stern lecture and allowed her to return home. Arrested again in July 1862, she was sent to Old Capitol Prison in Washington, D.C., where she remained for one month until exchanged. After being imprisoned again, she fled south and sailed to London, where she married. Boyd returned to America as an actress whose career spanned

only four years. She was married three times, and she died of a heart attack in 1900 while preparing to give a recital of her adventures to a group of Wisconsin veterans.

Jackson Earns a Nickname

"Look," Confederate General Barnard Bee is said to have cried to his fleeing soldiers during the First Battle of Bull Run, "**there stands Jackson like a stone wall. Rally behind the Virginians.**" Word of Bee's declaration to his troops reached Richmond papers, which were quick to christen General Thomas J. Jackson "Stonewall" and his troops the "Stonewall Brigade." Those close to Bee when he uttered those famous words, however, differed in their interpretation of his comments. **Some stated that the remarks were actually meant as an insult to Jackson due to his delay in committing his troops to the fight.** The true meaning will forever remain a mystery, for Bee was mortally wounded in the fight and never had a chance to clarify his remarks. There is no disagreement, however, that **Jackson—**

stern, deeply religious, and somewhat eccentric—justly earned his nickname and vast fame as the war progressed.

One of only two wartime photographs of Stonewall Jackson, this one was taken in 1862 in Winchester, Virginia, when he was visiting the home of his doctor, Hunter Holmes McGuire. One of McGuire's sisters suggested that Jackson have his image taken, so he went to a local photographer and sat for this portrait. His wife considered this the best photograph ever taken of her husband.

Top Ten Union Generals

Ulysses S. Grant   Primary Battles: Vicksburg, Shiloh, Petersburg
Aggressive; designed strategy that defeated Confederate armies

William T. Sherman   Primary Battles: Atlanta, March to the Sea
Excellent military strategist

Philip H. Sheridan   Primary Battles: Cedar Creek, Yellow Tavern, Five Forks
Great, fiery motivator and ruthless opponent

George Thomas   Primary Battles: Nashville, Chickamauga
The "Rock of Chickamauga"; a dependable and steady commander

George Meade   Primary Battle: Gettysburg
Won the greatest battle of the war after being given command only five days earlier

James McPherson   Primary Battle: Vicksburg, Atlanta Campaign
Although overly cautious at times, dependable army commander

Winfield S. Hancock   Primary Battles: Gettysburg, Overland Campaign
Recalled a staff member, "One felt safe when near him"

John Sedgwick   Primary Battles: Rappahannock Bridge, Spottsylvania
Handled his corps with tremendous skill

Gouverneur K. Warren   Primary Battles: Gettysburg, Overland Campaign
"Hero of Gettysburg" and victim of Sheridan's contempt

George A. Custer   Primary Battles: Gettysburg, Antietam Campaign
"Brave, dashing, enterprising"

Top Ten Confederate Generals

Robert E. Lee — Primary Battles: Seven Days, 2nd Bull Run, Chancellorsville, Fredericksburg
One of the most-loved and skillful generals in U.S. history

Thomas "Stonewall" Jackson — Primary Battles: 2nd Bull Run, Chancellorsville
Excellent tactician, great motivator

Albert S. Johnston — Primary Battle: Shiloh
President Davis said, "If Sidney Johnston is not a general . . . we have no generals"

Nathan B. Forrest — Primary Battles: Fort Pillow, Brices Cross Roads
Struck Union armies with "lightning blows"; excellent strategist

James Longstreet — Primary Battles: Chickamauga, Wilderness
Excellent tactician; faithful confidant of Lee

James E. B. Stuart — Primary Battles: Peninsula Campaign, Brandy Station
Bold to a point very close to recklessness; "eyes" of Army of Northern Virginia

Ambrose P. Hill — Primary Battles: Seven Days, Cedar Mountain
Excellent combat officer; hindered by psychosomatic illnesses; thought by Lee to be best major general in his army

Patrick Cleburne — Primary Battles: Murfreesboro, Chattanooga
Savage fighter and superb battlefield officer

D. H. Hill — Primary Battles: Big Bethel Church, Chickamauga
Distinguished battlefield commander

Robert E. Rodes — Primary Battles: South Mountain, Chancellorsville
One of the best division commanders in the Confederacy

Reports of massacres of black troops by Confederate forces surfaced throughout the later stages of the war. The most notable episode was during the capture of Fort Pillow, Tennessee, on April 13, 1864, where only 58 of 262 black soldiers survived the battle. Although Confederate forces insisted no massacre had taken place, General Nathan Bedford Forrest, the commanding officer, himself wrote, "The river was dyed with blood of the slaughtered for 200 yards."

This is a portion of the notorious **prison camp at Anderson-ville.** Located in southwestern Georgia, this 16-acre site received its first Northern prisoners in February 1864. **Almost 13,000 prisoners died there by the war's end just over a year later, due primarily to malnutrition and disease.**

Opened in May 1864, the **Elmira prison** became notorious for the conditions its Confederate inmates were forced to endure. These wooden barracks were erected to replace tents as winter approached, but they failed to ease a **prisoner death rate of nearly 25 percent** during its time of operation.

Louisa May Alcott, the writer of *Little Women,* served as a nurse for the Union during the Civil War. After about a month and a half, though, she became gravely ill from typhoid. The consummate writer, she detailed her experiences in *Hospital Sketches.* She wrote, "The house had been a hotel before hospitals were needed, and many of the doors still bore their old names; some not so inappropriate as might be imagined, for my ward was in truth a ball-room, if gunshot wounds could christen it. Forty beds were prepared, many already tenanted by tired men who fell down anywhere, and drowsed till the smell of food roused them. Round the great stove was gathered the dreariest group I ever saw—ragged, gaunt and pale, mud to the knees, with bloody bandages untouched since put on days before; many bundled up in blankets, coats being lost or useless; and all wearing that disheartened look which proclaimed defeat, more plainly than any telegram of the Burnside blunder."

Civil War Challenge

Q: Which two presidents who served after the Civil War had owned slaves before the conflict?

A: Andrew Johnson and Ulysses S. Grant

Postwar reunions of soldiers began in the 1880s and added to the idea of national reconciliation after the Civil War and Reconstruction. A few tentative reunions of former adversaries blossomed into more frequent joint get-togethers. Survivors of the Philadelphia Brigade and Pickett's division held a joint reunion at Gettysburg in 1887, the aged veterans shaking hands across the stone wall where 24 years earlier they had shot and stabbed each other in fury. The Union vets below marched in 1905, 40 years after the end of hostilities.

Called by his friend Abraham Lincoln "the greatest little man I ever met," **Colonel Ephraim Elmer Ellsworth became the North's first martyr of the war.** Before the war, Ellsworth studied law in Lincoln's office and was celebrated for leading a national championship drill team called the U.S. Zouave Cadets. At the outbreak of the war, he recruited a regiment—largely from New York City's fire department—that he patterned after his drill team. "I want men who can go into a fight now," he reasoned.

Clothed in colorful Zouave uniforms based on a French army design, his regiment was among the first to reach Washington. On May 24, 1861, the day after Virginia officially seceded from the Union, Ellsworth led his men to seize Alexandria, Virginia. Spying a rebel flag flying atop a hotel, he entered the building, climbed to the roof, and tore the flag down. Descending the stairs, he was shot to death by the innkeeper, who in turn was killed by one of Ellsworth's soldiers. The Union martyr's body lay in state at the White House, where a grieving Lincoln led the nation in mourning.

When **General Joseph Johnston** was wounded at the Battle of Seven Pines, Jefferson Davis appointed Robert E. Lee to replace him in the command of the Army of Northern Virginia. Of his wounding and Lee's subsequent appointment, Johnston commented, **"The shot that struck me down is the very best that has been fired for the Southern cause yet."** The wisdom of his words was soon borne out, much to the Union's misfortune.

The Ultimate Symbol of Reunion

As **General William T. Sherman's** army pushed south toward Atlanta, it was met on several battlefields by rebels under the command of General Joseph Johnston. Unable to stop the Union advance, Johnston was relieved of his command.

But following the cessation of hostilities, the two opponents became cordial friends. **When Sherman died on February 14, 1891, Johnston walked next to the casket as an honorary pallbearer.** He fell victim to pneumonia in the days following the funeral and died on March 21.

Battle of Chancellorsville

On May 1, 1863, Union General Joseph Hooker amassed 134,000 troops around the Chancellor House against less than half that many Confederates commanded by Robert E. Lee. But these superior numbers were useless when pitted against the genius and fighting skills of Lee and his army, who inflicted one of the worst defeats of the war on the hapless Union army. Taking advantage of the lightly defended federal right flank, Stonewall Jackson secretly marched his troops around the enemy front and struck the Union 11th Corps. Over the next few days Hooker's forces fought for their lives until safely across the Rappahannock River. The Confederate victory, however, was offset by Jackson's fatal wounding. Mistakenly shot by his own side, Jackson died on May 10, 1863. Informed of the death of his brilliant general, Lee said, "I have lost my right arm."

"Let us cross over the river, and rest under the shade of the trees."

—Stonewall Jackson's dying words

Newspaper editors throughout the country were targets of mob action if their papers printed material that was contrary to local opinion. This illustration from *Frank Leslie's Illustrated Newspaper* depicts a **Northern editor being tarred and feathered for printing pro-Southern sentiments.** Several times during the war, newspaper offices were ransacked and editors thrown out of town.

On the night of March 5, 1863, soldiers from the 2nd Ohio Cavalry, who were camped outside of Columbus, Ohio, attacked the office of a local newspaper. The *Crisis* had printed antiarmy stories denigrating Ohio soldiers. Local police were "persuaded" to remain aloof from the fray until the angry troops exacted their revenge.

In June of that year, Union General Ambrose Burnside shut down the *Chicago Times* for "repeated expression of disloyal and incendiary sentiments." This paper had called emancipation "a criminal wrong" and had become anti-Lincoln, antiblack, and antiwar. Lincoln, although he understood Burnside's actions, rescinded the general's order three days later and allowed the paper to continue publishing.

Although an advocate of free speech, President Lincoln at times allowed the suppression of newspapers when a paper willingly misrepresented government policy or became rabidly antigovernment. The President also had the power to arrest editors after the writ of habeas corpus was suspended.

Steps to Load an Infantry Musket

1. Place the musket on the ground, barrel up.
2. Use your teeth to tear open a paper cartridge containing gunpowder and a lead ball.
3. Pour the powder and ball into the muzzle of the musket.
4. Ram the charge down the barrel with a ramrod.
5. Replace the ramrod.
6. Half cock the musket's hammer, and place a percussion cap on the nipple under the hammer.
7. Fully cock the hammer, aim, and fire.

The American-made Springfield rifle was the most widely used firearm during the war. Its rifled bore, interchangeable parts, and conical ammunition set it apart from guns used in earlier conflicts.

Causes of Death in the Union Army

Cause	Officers	Enlisted	Total
Killed or died of wounds	6,365	103,705	110,070
Disease	2,712	197,008	199,720
Accidents	142	3,972	4,114
Drowning	106	4,838	4,944
Sunstroke	5	308	313
Murder	37	483	520
Killed after capture	14	90	104
Suicide	26	365	391
Military execution	0	267	267
Executed by the enemy	4	60	64
While in Confederate prisons	83	24,783	24,866
Causes known, but not specified	62	1,972	2,034
Cause not stated	28	12,093	12,121
Totals	9,584	349,944	359,528

No accurate accounting of Confederates' cause of death exists due to the lack of documentation after the war.

On June 10, 1864, General Sherman's army faced Confederate entrenchments on Kennesaw Mountain northwest of Marietta, Georgia. He decided on a frontal attack against the rebel position on June 27. "Our losses were heavy indeed," one of Sherman's corps commanders wrote, "and our gain was nothing. We realized now, as never before, the futility of direct assaults upon intrenched lines already well prepared and well manned."

John Bell Hood

Like the commander himself, General John Bell Hood's Confederate army was crippled almost beyond repair following the fall of Atlanta, Georgia, on September 1, 1864. By November, when Hood led his army into Tennessee, combat wounds had cost him a leg and the use of an arm. His army was destroyed at the Battle of Nashville on December 15th and 16th. Hood resigned his command a few weeks later.

While President Abraham Lincoln congratulated **General George Meade** for his victory at Gettysburg, he was critical of his general's failure to take advantage of the win and to crush Robert E. Lee's army before it could limp back into Virginia. **Lincoln likened Meade's failure to pursue Lee to "an old woman shooing geese across a creek."**

"I was born and bred on the plantation of Old Mars Robert English, one hundred miles from Charleston. My younger days were happy ones. I played with the massa's children until I became seven or eight years old, then I had to go into the field with the other black folks and work hard all day from earliest dawn till late at night. We ate twice a day, that is, when we got up in the morning we were driven out into the fields and were called into breakfast at noon by the blast of an old tin horn.

"All we got to eat then was three corn cake dumplins and one plate of soup. No meat unless there happened to be a rotten piece in the smoke house. This would be given to us to make our soup. Why the dogs got better eating than we poor colored folks. We would go out into the fields again and work very hard until dark, when we were driven in by the crack of the overseer's lash and frequently that crack meant blood from some unfortunate creature's back, who, becoming weary had shown signs of faltering."

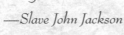

—Slave John Jackson

In response to the use of black troops to bolster the Union army, Jefferson Davis approved a policy that called for the execution of any white Union officer commanding black soldiers. But in an ironic attempt to bolster its own troop shortage, the Confederate Congress passed legislation in March 1865 calling for the enlistment of 300,000 black troops. This last-ditch effort proved too late to save their cause.

Members of Company E, 4th U.S. Colored Troops pose at Fort Lincoln, one of the many strongholds surrounding Washington, D.C., throughout the war.

George E. Pickett

George E. Pickett's division of Virginians
was all but destroyed in the last major
action of the Battle of Gettysburg.
On the third day of the battle,
Pickett's Charge—one of the
worst military disasters of the
Civil War—collapsed at a copse
of trees on Cemetery Ridge. Historian John B. Bachelder first
referred to these trees as the "High
Water Mark of the Confederacy," a
name that has stuck. Confederate troops would never mount this
kind of invasion again.

While on the march, soldiers of both sides ate limited rations, often hastily prepared. In camp, however, **company cooks** assumed that food preparation duty. "These cooks," one veteran later recalled, **"were men selected from the company, who had a taste or an ambition for the business."**

Pre-War Occupations of Union Soldiers

Occupation	Percentage
Farmer	48%
Mechanic	24%
Laborer	16%
Commercial Pursuit	5%
Professional	3%
Miscellaneous	4%

The 1863 Federal Draft Act proved to be a horrendous failure. In New York City, about 13 percent of the males who were called failed to report for induction. More than 55 percent of those who did report were given exemptions. The draft resulted in the induction of 35,882 soldiers, with all but 9,880 being substitutes. Subsequent drafts in 1864 were no more successful.

Mobs of draft protesters roamed the streets of New York City for three days, beginning on July 13, 1863, **fighting pitched battles with police.** Union troops and artillery, fresh from victory at Gettysburg, were called in to restore order. In the end, **more than 70 people were killed, hundreds more were injured, and property damage exceeded $1.5 million.**

Chapter 4

"It Is Well That War Is So Terrible"

"It is well that war is so terrible—we should grow too fond of it."

—General Robert E. Lee

Having formed his line in the predawn hours of May 12, 1864, Union General Winfield Hancock launched 20,000 troops against the Confederate Mule Shoe outside of Spotsylvania Court House, Virginia. Although the Union soldiers took the position, Confederate reinforcements reclaimed it later in the day.

Following the battle, Generals Grant and Meade and their staffs stopped at Massaponax Church, where Grant had the pews brought into the yard under two shade trees. In this photo, he leans over Meade's right shoulder, pointing out a position on a map.

Clara Barton

Clara Barton, **founder of the American Red Cross,** led a volunteer effort to assist wounded soldiers after the First Battle of Bull Run. The surgeon general later granted her a pass to travel with army ambulances "for the purpose of distributing comforts for the sick and wounded, and for nursing them." Barton served in this capacity in Virginia, Maryland, and South Carolina, attracting national attention for her efforts. **In addition to caring for the sick and wounded, she visited returning prisoners of war to learn the fate of men missing in action so their families could be contacted.**

Ulysses S. Grant

"He was possessed of a moral and physical courage," wrote Horace Porter, an aide and friend of Ulysses S. Grant, "which was equal to every emergency in which he was placed. He was calm amid excitement, patient under trials, sure in judgment, clear in foresight, never depressed by reverses or unduly elated by success. . . . His singular self-reliance enabled him at critical junctures to decide instantly questions of vital moment without dangerous delay in seeking advice from others, and to assume the gravest responsibilities without asking any one to share them."

Born April 27, 1822, in Point Pleasant, Ohio, Grant was baptized Hiram Ulysses Grant. He assumed the name Ulysses Simpson after a member of Congress mistakenly listed that name on Grant's admission papers to West Point. Graduating from the academy in 1843, 21st in his class, he entered the infantry and served with distinction during the Mexican War. After a transfer to the Pacific Northwest, he became severely depressed by the isolation of his remote post and the loneliness of being away from his wife, Julia, and two children. This caused him to turn to drink and marked the beginning of his reputation as a drunkard. When he failed to secure a transfer east, he resigned his commission in 1854. Over the next six years, he jumped from one failed business venture to another, finally accepting a job as a clerk in his father's leather goods store. Shortly after the war began, he secured a commission as colonel in the 21st Illinois Volunteer Infantry Regiment.

A string of victories in the Western Theater throughout the war resulted in Lincoln naming him commander of all Union forces in the spring of 1864. Waging a war of attrition on all fronts, he led the Northern army to victory.

Grant rode the crest of his fame after the war to the presidency in 1868. He served two terms that

were marked by scandal and corruption. Once again unlucky in business after the presidency, Grant was forced into bankruptcy. With only his military pension to subsist on, Grant began writing his memoirs to support his family, finishing the project shortly before his death from throat cancer on July 23, 1885.

Regimental Mascots

Many regiments brought along or acquired mascots who helped the soldiers pass the time in camp and generated regimental pride in time of battle. In the Union army, for example, the 11th and the 102nd Pennsylvania Infantries each had bull  terriers, Sallie and Dog Jack, respectively. Neither survived the war—Sallie was killed in battle, and Dog Jack disappeared from camp. **The 8th Wisconsin Infantry had Old Abe,** shown here, **a pet eagle that perched atop a specially made platform carried alongside the regimental color guard.** Old Abe flew above the troops of the 8th Wisconsin during many of its battles. During its service in Louisiana, the 159th New York Infantry acquired a black bear cub that loved to wrestle with the soldiers and drink from their canteens. The bear went along by ship to Virginia in 1864, survived the Shenandoah Valley Campaign, and marched in the Grand Review.

The 8th Wisconsin's Old Abe also survived the war. His remains were stuffed and put on display in the Wisconsin state capitol in Madison until fire destroyed the building (and Old Abe) in 1904.

Civil War Challenge

The Battle of Gettysburg

1. What were the dates of the battle?
2. Who was the Confederate cavalry commander who failed to warn Lee of the Union army's position?
3. Who was the commander of the 20th Maine Volunteer Infantry?
4. Whose Union cavalry division held off the Confederate advance on the first day of the battle until the arrival of the First Corps?
5. Who moved his Union corps, against orders, out of position on the second afternoon of the battle?

Civil War Challenge Answers

1. July 1, July 2, and July 3, 1863
2. General James Ewell Brown "Jeb" Stuart
3. Colonel Joshua Chamberlain
4. General John Buford
5. General Daniel Sickles

Unsupported by gold and with few printing restrictions, paper money flowed from national, state, and local presses. Banks, railroads, and private businesses often issued their own currency.

Battlefield Preservation

Civil War preservationists are in the midst of their own war. While conquering enemies was the ultimate goal in the Civil War itself, control of land was the means to that end. Control of land is also the objective of this modern war. Preservation of America's heritage and the battlefields over which soldiers

fought and died is the ultimate goal. Organizations such as the Civil War Preservation Trust, Friends of Gettysburg, and the Battle of Nashville Preservation Society solicit private funds to purchase land before it falls victim to bulldozers and architects. Without their effort, thousands of acres of historically significant land are taken away from future generations of historians.

The 1864 Democratic presidential ticket, shown on this Currier & Ives poster, consisted of George McClellan and George H. Pendleton. More favorable news from the battlefront in 1864 enabled President Abraham Lincoln to be reelected with 55 percent of the popular vote.

Cedar Creek

After decisive victories at Winchester, Virginia (September 19, 1864), and Fisher's Hill (September 21–22, 1864), Union General Philip Sheridan was convinced that his Shenandoah Valley Campaign was over. Confederate General Jubal A. Early's Army of the Valley District, 18,000 strong, had suffered almost 5,000 casualties in those two battles and had lost a large portion of its vital supplies as it fled down the valley. Sheridan set up his camp north of Cedar Creek. When Confederate reinforcements arrived to raise his strength to 21,000, Early studied Sheridan's position, looking for and finding a weakness in an unprotected Union left flank resting on the creek. Early struck the exposed flank at dawn on October 19. Caught totally by surprise, the federal line collapsed. Sheridan, absent at the beginning of the battle, raced down the Valley Turnpike from Winchester once he heard the boom of cannons. His appearance rallied his army, and he launched a counterattack. When the smoke cleared, 5,600 Union troops and 2,900 Confederate casualties were left on the field while the rebels fled south.

Cedar Creek Battlefield

When General Philip Sheridan reached Cedar Creek, Virginia, on the morning of October 19, the rebel surprise attack had already routed his army. He wrote in his memoirs that, as his command formed for a counterattack, he passed along the entire length of his line waving his hat. In this illustration he waves a flag instead.

More than 300 acres of the land over which this important battle was fought have recently been acquired by the National Park Service and include the Belle Grove Plantation and the Stephen Dodson Ramseur Monument, but the serenity of the location is in peril. Plans have been made to widen both Interstate 81 and an exit that runs adjacent to the park.

Homestead Act of 1862

When Southern states seceded from the Union, their representatives withdrew from Congress. This left Northern legislators, overwhelmingly Republican, in the position to pass pet projects and bills previously defeated or vetoed. The Federal Homestead Act, for example, was passed on May 20, 1862, and allowed the free distribution of public lands west of the Mississippi for settlement. Settlers secured title to a quarter section of land (160 acres) if they paid a legal fee of $10 and lived there and made improvements for five years.

Homesteaders in Custer County, Nebraska

Types of Period Photographs

In addition to views of generals and battlefield vistas, photographers captured the likenesses of many of the soldiers of both sides on the carte de visite (visiting card), a $2\frac{1}{2} \times 4$-inch cardboard stock featuring a mounted portrait on one side and the photographer's mark on the back. Soldiers often sent copies to loved ones at home. Tens of thousands of these photographs have survived, forever capturing the images of young men who suffered the many hardships of war.

Boys, some not yet teenagers, were not an uncommon sight aboard naval vessels. This lad poses next to a cannon on the deck of the USS *New Hampshire*.

Influential Civil War Movies

(in chronological order)

Movie	Year	Director
The Birth of a Nation	1915	D. W. Griffith
Gone With the Wind	1939	Victor Fleming
The Red Badge of Courage	1951	John Huston
Friendly Persuasion	1956	William Wyler
The Horse Soldiers	1959	John Ford
Shenandoah	1965	Andrew V. McLaglen
Glory	1989	Edward Zwick
Gettysburg	1993	Ronald F. Maxwell
Gods and Generals	2003	Ronald F. Maxwell
Cold Mountain	2003	Anthony Minghella

Originally appearing as a serial in the Washington *National Era* in 1851, ***Uncle Tom's Cabin*** was published in book form in 1852. More than 300,000 copies of the book were sold within its first year of publication. It was even **more popular in England, where one million copies were sold within a year.**

Chickamauga

Union General William Rosecrans executed a brilliant tactical maneuver to drive Confederate General Braxton Bragg's Army of Tennessee from the strategic communication center of Chattanooga, Tennessee, on September 8, 1863. Five days later, 58,000 Union troops pursued Bragg's 66,000-strong command south into Georgia. General George Thomas attacked on the morning of September 19, but by nightfall, neither army had gained a significant advantage. Confederate troops struck the next morning at 9:30, driving most of the Union troops from the field by noon. Nevertheless, Thomas's command held off the rebels to protect Rosecrans's retreat to Chattanooga. More than 16,000 Union and 18,000 Confederate casualties fell during the battle. For his stubborn defense, Thomas gained the nickname "Rock of Chickamauga." Contrary to the desires of his subordinates, Bragg failed to pursue the retreating enemy.

Chickamauga and Chattanooga National Military Park

Union and Confederate veterans established the Chickamauga Memorial Association in 1889. A year later, Congress declared this land set aside "for the purpose of preserving and suitably marking for historical and professional military study the fields of some of the most remarkable maneuvers and brilliant fighting of the war of rebellion." Five years later, this first national military park was dedicated. The visitor to the site will find 666 monuments, 257 cannons, and 659 markers deployed across more than 8,000 acres of the Chickamauga and Chattanooga battlefields. The site was turned over to the National Park Service in 1933. Points of interest include:

Snodgrass Hill   Adolph Ochs Museum

Point Park   Signal Point Reservation

Orchard Knob

Chattanooga

Following its defeat at the Battle of Chickamauga, Union General William Rosecrans's Army of the Cumberland became trapped in Chattanooga, Tennessee, by the rain-swollen Tennessee River to its north and west and by Confederate General Braxton Bragg's Army of Tennessee strung out along the dominating heights of Missionary Ridge to the south and east. Receiving word that Rosecrans planned to withdraw from Chattanooga, Ulysses S. Grant replaced him with George H. Thomas. Union troops soon opened a single rail line (the "Cracker Line") to replenish the supplies of the besieged army. With the arrival of reinforcements, Grant, who assumed overall command after arriving in Chattanooga, planned his attack. Having sent more than 20,000 soldiers toward the Union stronghold at Knoxville, Bragg found himself outnumbered by that same number as Grant launched his offensive. On November 24, in a fight that literally took place above the clouds, Union General Joseph Hooker led 10,000 against 7,000 of Bragg's soldiers perched atop Lookout Mountain. Hooker took the position, losing about 500 to the Confederates' 1,200. The next day, the remaining Confederate defenders were driven from Missionary Ridge at a cost of 6,700 Confederate and 6,000 Union casualties.

"It seems as if it could not be that I have to spend this day her[e] & Mr C in the army. . . . My God protect him & bring him safely back. . . . O! It seems so dreadful to be thus separated. If he only be spared to come home again that we may yet long live together I will not murmur at this cruel separation. The great sin of slavery has brought all this calamity on us—God grant us grace & strength for our day & trial."

—Rachel Cormany, writing in her diary on the third anniversary of her marriage to Samuel Cormany, who served in the 16th Pennsylvania Cavalry

This painting, *War Spirit at Home*, captures life on the home front. Although the children celebrate the news of Grant's victory at Vicksburg, the women carry the heavy burden of war.

Payment

At the start of the war, **Confederate volunteers were paid 11 dollars per month.** Even though rampant inflation lowered the value of the Confederate dollar, it wasn't until **1864 that the monthly payment was increased to 18 dollars.** Not only was this amount of money next to **worthless due to inflation,** but soldiers **had to wait months before they even received it.** "Yesterday we were paid up—wages to Jany. 1, 1864 and commutation for clothing for the year ending Oct. 8, 1863," observed a rebel soldier. "As the 'old issue' of Confederate notes will soon be worthless, it seems the Treasury Department is very anxious to get rid of it—hence the large installment of wages we received."

This Confederate infantry private is well clad as his photo is taken, but as the war lengthened, the Confederate army suffered severe shortages.

Items from a **typical mess kit** included a small pot with lid, the top of a canteen with its cork stopper, eating utensils, a collapsible cup, and the haversack or ration bag.

Construction of a new dome on the Capitol was authorized by Congress in 1855 but had not been completed when the Civil War began. In 1862, President Lincoln ordered the construction to be continued as "a sign we intend the Union shall go on." To echoes of a 35-gun salute (one for each state, both North and South), the dome was completed on December 2, 1863. It is capped by a bronze statue of Freedom.

Civil War Challenge

While Union soldiers usually named battles after topo-
graphical features, often bodies of water, Confederates
used names of nearby towns. Match the Union name of
each of the following battles with its Confederate name:

Union Name	Confederate Name
Antietam	Oak Hills
Bull Run	Murfreesboro
Pea Ridge	Fort Loudon
Opequon Creek	Winchester
Pittsburg Landing	Manassas
Fort Sanders	Sharpsburg
Ocean Pond	Elkhorn Tavern
Stones River	Shiloh
Monitor & Merrimack	Olustee
Wilson's Creek	Monitor & Virginia

Civil War Challenge Answers

Union Name	Confederate Name
Antietam	Sharpsburg
Bull Run	Manassas
Pea Ridge	Elkhorn Tavern
Opequon Creek	Winchester
Pittsburg Landing	Shiloh
Fort Sanders	Fort Loudon
Ocean Pond	Olustee
Stones River	Murfreesboro
Monitor & Merrimack	Monitor & Virginia
Wilson's Creek	Oak Hills

A number of men claimed to be **the last living Civil War soldier,** but once the wheat was separated from the chaff, the last bona fide veteran appears to have been **Albert Woolson, who died at age 108 on August 2, 1956.** He enlisted as a drummer boy in the 1st Minnesota Heavy Artillery during the last year of the war. Although his unit was garrisoned at Chattanooga, Tennessee, from late 1864 until mid-1865, it saw no action. After the war, Woolson lived in Duluth, Minnesota. Even in old age, he proudly wore his Union uniform into classrooms, carrying his drum and telling youngsters about his experiences during the war.

"There is nothing left me but to go and see General Grant, and I had rather die a thousand deaths."

—Robert E. Lee,
prior to his ride to Appomattox Court House

Henry Ward Beecher

Brother of *Uncle Tom's Cabin* author Harriet Beecher Stowe, Henry Ward Beecher was himself an outspoken critic of slavery. A minister by profession, he was equally critical of radical and fanatical abolitionists. He called John Brown's disastrous raid on the federal arsenal at Harpers Ferry the "act of a crazy old man."

Born in Litchfield, Connecticut, in 1813, Beecher had a knack for oratory and theatrics that helped attract public attention to his antislavery message. He once held a fake slave auction at Boston's Plymouth Church to raise funds to free two young girls.

A gifted writer, Beecher continued to encourage an end to slavery throughout the early years of the war. After the fighting ended, he supported readmitting the Southern states quickly. He continued to champion humanitarian causes until his death in 1887.

Civil War reenactments became bigger and better in the 1970s, and by the 1980s and 1990s, large-scale reenactments sometimes involved more than 10,000 participants. The reenacting community includes participants from all walks of life who purchase everything they need—such as period eyeglasses with prescription lenses to hardtack crackers—from a number of specialized businesses.

In Winslow Homer's *Prisoners from the Front,* a Union general examines a group of captured Southern prisoners escorted by a Union guard. The young boy and old man are indicative of the range of ages serving in the Confederate armies.

The **camp cook** didn't have the most sophisticated tools with which to do his work, but a **coffee pot was one of the primary weapons in his arsenal.** "It was coffee at meals and between meals," remembered a soldier, "and men going on guard or coming off guard drank it all hours of the night." At least that was true in the Northern army. **Confederates** weren't so lucky. They **rarely had coffee in sufficient quantities to meet demand, which made it a prime commodity to seek in trade from Billy Yank whenever the opportunity arose.**

Five Forks

Confederate Generals George Pickett and Fitzhugh Lee, Robert E. Lee's nephew, accepted invitations to attend a fish bake on April 1, 1865. They were glad to break the monotony of overseeing the protection of Five Forks, Virginia, a town with immense importance to the rebel defense of Petersburg. The five roads that passed through the town were a key communication link between Lee's army and what was left of the Confederacy. While Pickett and Fitzhugh Lee were away, Union General Philip Sheridan's 27,000 soldiers attacked the 10,000 defenders. The rebels were routed, leaving behind 4,500 casualties to 1,000 for the Union. Once Five Forks fell into the hands of Union troops, the fate of the Confederate Army of Northern Virginia was sealed. Robert E. Lee surrendered eight days later at Appomattox Court House, Virginia.

The **balloon *Intrepid*,** shown here being inflated, was one of seven military observation balloons approved by the U.S. government in August 1861. Such balloons were used by both sides to **keep track of military movements early in the war.** But although the "aeronauts" could supply instant intelligence from unobstructed heights of several hundred feet, **the old-fashioned generals did not trust their observations.** Thaddeus Lowe commanded the fledgling balloon corps until May 1863, when he resigned due to lack of support from military leaders.

The Zouaves were a distinctive group of soldiers. Units from both the North and South adopted this unique style of uniform, inspired by French soldiers in Northern Africa. French Zouaves gained a significant reputation as ferocious fighters in both the Crimean and Franco-Prussian wars and sparked something of a fad on American shores. Elmer Ellsworth recruited a drill team dressed in the Zouave style in Chicago in 1859 and toured 20 cities before the war. At the war's outbreak, a number of units took the style into actual combat.

Chapter 5

"Mine Eyes Have Seen the Glory"

A Union and a Confederate soldier

fight for the standard in this painting

by an unknown artist.

"The Battle Hymn of the Republic"

by Julia Ward Howe

Mine eyes have seen the glory of the
coming of the Lord;
He is trampling out the vintage
where the grapes of wrath are
stored;
He hath loosed the fateful lightning
of his terrible swift sword,
His truth is marching on.

(Chorus)

Glory, Glory Hallelujah,
Glory, Glory Hallelujah,
Glory, Glory Hallelujah,
His truth is marching on.

I have seen Him in the watch fires
of a hundred circling camps;

They have builded Him an altar in
the evening dews and damps;
I can read his righteous sentence by
the dim and flaring lamps,
His day is marching on.

(Chorus)

I have read a fiery gospel writ in
burnished rows of steel:
"As ye deal with My condemners, so
with you My Grace shall deal;
Let the Hero, born of woman, crush
the serpent with his heel,
Since God is marching on."

(Chorus)

He has sounded forth the trumpet
that shall never call retreat;
He is sifting out the hearts of men
before His Judgment Seat;
Oh! be swift, my soul, to answer
Him, be jubilant, my feet!
Our God is marching on.

(Chorus)

In the beauty of the lilies Christ was
born across the sea,
With a glory in his bosom that
transfigures you and me;
As He died to make men holy, let us
die to make men free,
While God is marching on.

(Chorus)

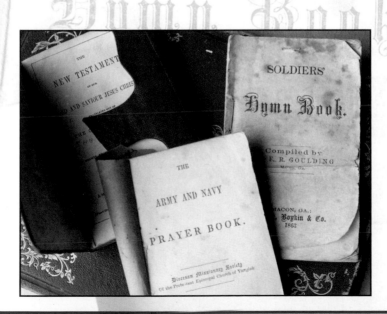

Nicknamed "Fighting Joe" for his performance in the Battle of Williamsburg, Virginia, in May 1862, **General Joseph Hooker** replaced General Ambrose Burnside in command of the Army of the Potomac in January 1863. **He devised a brilliant plan to steal a march on Robert E. Lee near Chancellorsville, Virginia.** He was at the brink of success, **but his moral courage failed him when Lee's army stood and fought instead of retreating.** Turning the initiative over to Lee, Hooker was decisively defeated. This caused Lincoln to lament, "My God! My God! What will the country say." Hooker later wrote, "To tell the truth, I just lost confidence in Joe Hooker."

Civil War Firsts

First organized care of wounded on the battlefield

First naval mines or "torpedoes"

First military draft in the United States

First income tax

First photograph taken in combat

First ironclad ships

First use of portable telegraph units on the battlefield

First submarine used to sink an enemy ship

First repeating rifle used in combat

First Gatling gun

On the evening of July 18, 1863, a Union column stormed Fort Wagner, which overlooked Charleston Harbor. Colonel Robert G. Shaw and his 54th Massachusetts, made up of free blacks and runaway slaves, led the assault. Southern defenders repelled the poorly planned and executed assault, inflicting more than 1,500 casualties.

"Whole lines of battle rushed up to their beloved chief and struggled with each other to wring him once more by hand. Not an eye that looked on that scene was dry."

—A witness, describing Robert E. Lee's return to his command after his surrender to Ulysses S. Grant

Civil War Challenge

Battles of Lookout Mountain and Missionary Ridge

1. What was the name given to the route Ulysses S. Grant used to provide supplies to the troops in Chattanooga?
2. Identify another name for the Battle of Lookout Mountain.
3. Whose divisions were given the order to attack the Confederate defenses on the mountain?
4. Who won the Congressional Medal of Honor for his heroics on the slopes of Missionary Ridge? (His son would also win the Medal of Honor.)
5. What Confederate division commander, whose troops defended Lookout Mountain, was nicknamed "the Stonewall Jackson of the West"?

Civil War Challenge Answers

1. The Cracker Line
2. Battle Above the Clouds
3. Joseph Hooker
4. First Lieutenant Arthur McArthur
5. Confederate General Patrick Cleburne

The haversack was one item many soldiers on both sides found essential. Measuring about a foot square, the canvas sack had a waterproof coating and was designed to hold all sorts of things. "After they had been in use for a few weeks," recalled a Union soldier, "[they were used] as a receptacle for chunks of fat meat, damp sugar tied up in a rag, broken crackers and bread, with a lump of cheese or two."

Children at War

The Wounded Drummer Boy
by Eastman Johnson

Almost half of the more than two million Union soldiers were under the age of 19. Lax enlistment standards and indifferent examination techniques allowed easy access for underage recruits. More than 800,000 youth who enlisted were only 16 or 17 years old. Approximately 100,000 were "no more than 15," according to a postwar study.

Boys 16 years and under could officially enlist as musicians. Often during battle they would set their instruments aside to bear stretchers and aid the wounded. The war's most celebrated youngster, 12-year-old Johnny Clem, served with the 22nd Michigan Infantry and shot a Confederate officer at the Battle of Chickamauga.

> *"We must destroy this army of Grant's before it gets to the James River."*
>
> —*General Robert E. Lee, Spring 1864*

It took about eight hours on June 14, 1864, for Grant's engineers to span the James River with a pontoon bridge of more than 2,000 feet anchored in the middle by three schooners. The Union Army of the Potomac began crossing the river later that night.

Kennesaw Mountain

Once Union General William Sherman launched the advance of his 100,000-troop army from Chattanooga, Tennessee, toward Atlanta, Georgia, on May 5, 1864, Confederate General Joseph Johnston repeatedly used the Georgia terrain to place his 60,000 soldiers in strong defensive positions. Sherman was able to maneuver around the rebels for more than a month until he reached Kennesaw Mountain on June 10, where he was forced to launch a frontal attack, sending 16,000 troops charging up the mountain on June 27. Four hours later, after losing more than 2,000, the general halted the assault. The Confederates, losing about 500, remained entrenched on the mountain, stalling Sherman's advance. Five days later, Sherman moved his army around Johnston's left flank and forced the rebels off the mountain.

Kennesaw Mountain National Battlefield Park

Union veterans of the battle successfully lobbied the state of Illinois to purchase 60 acres on a portion of the Kennesaw battlefield, where the state erected the Illinois Monument, dedicated on June 17, 1914. Almost three years later, Illinois passed the land to the U.S. Congress. While 2,884 acres have been incorporated into the park, another 10,000 acres are historically significant and are disappearing at an alarming rate to the point where much of the park's boundary is adjacent to housing developments. More than 160,000 cars travel through the park each day.

George Gordon Meade

With the Confederate army roaming freely through Pennsylvania in late June 1863, Abraham Lincoln needed quickly to replace General Joseph Hooker, who had resigned as commander of the Army of the Potomac on June 27. Although General George G. Meade was initially reluctant to assume the responsibilities of army command, Lincoln's call to duty left him little choice in the matter. Meade was a deliberate, competent fighter who followed orders—all qualities Lincoln felt had been missing in Hooker and were essential to defeat General Robert E. Lee.

Meade was born in Cadiz, Spain, on December 31, 1815, while his father was overseas as a naval agent for the United States. He graduated from West Point in 1835, and most of his military service before the start of the war was as an engineer.

He was appointed a brigadier general of Pennsylvania volunteer troops in August 1861. His command joined George McClellan's Army of the Potomac in June 1862 and participated in the later stages of the Virginia Peninsula Campaign, during which Meade was wounded in the arm and the hip.

By June 1863, Meade had risen to the command of the 5th Corps. He had no aspirations to command the Army of the Potomac, but his strong dedication to duty made it impossible for him to decline the appointment when Lincoln offered it.

After his great victory at Gettysburg, Meade was criticized by Lincoln for allowing Lee's army to escape into Virginia. "My dear general," the President wrote, "I do not believe you appreciate the magnitude of the misfortune involved in Lee's escape. . . . Your golden opportunity is gone, and I am distressed immeasurably because of it."

It was no coincidence that Ulysses S. Grant established his headquarters with Meade's army when he assumed command of all Union armies the next spring. While Meade's superiors had confidence in his ability to fight, they lacked faith in his capacity to wage a successful campaign. Indeed, by the end of the war, Meade was little more than a figurehead, eclipsed by Grant's other lieutenants, Generals William Sherman and Philip Sheridan.

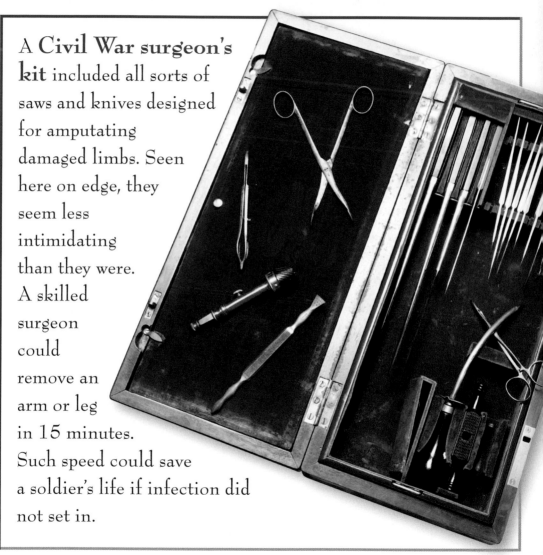

A **Civil War surgeon's kit** included all sorts of saws and knives designed for amputating damaged limbs. Seen here on edge, they seem less intimidating than they were. A skilled surgeon could remove an arm or leg in 15 minutes. Such speed could save a soldier's life if infection did not set in.

Civil War Challenge

Match the nickname with the person.

Nickname	Person
Rail Splitter	Union General William Sherman
Extra Billy	Confederate General William Jackson
Young Napoleon	Confederate General William Smith
Stonewall	Confederate General David Jones
Mudwall	Union General George Thomas
Shanks	Union General George McClellan
Old Brains	President Abraham Lincoln
Uncle Billy	Union General Henry Halleck
Rock of Chickamauga	Confederate General Thomas Jackson
Neighbor	Confederate General Nathan Evans

Civil War Challenge
Answers

Nickname	Person
Rail Splitter	President Abraham Lincoln
Extra Billy	Confederate General William Smith
Young Napoleon	Union General George McClellan
Stonewall	Confederate General Thomas Jackson
Mudwall	Confederate General William Jackson
Shanks	Confederate General Nathan Evans
Old Brains	Union General Henry Halleck
Uncle Billy	Union General William Sherman
Rock of Chickamauga	Union General George Thomas
Neighbor	Confederate General David Jones

An ironclad, 50-foot-long, cigar-shaped torpedo boat, the **CSS *David*** guarded the waters off Charleston, South Carolina. Several crafts of similar design were constructed to defend the inland and coastal waters of the Confederacy. **The semisubmersible vessels were such a threat to Union ships that Rear Admiral John A. Dahlgren offered a cash reward for their capture or destruction.**

"As the smoke was lifted by the gentle May breeze, one lone soldier advanced, bravely bearing the flag toward the breast works. At least a hundred men took deliberate aim at him, and fired at pointblank

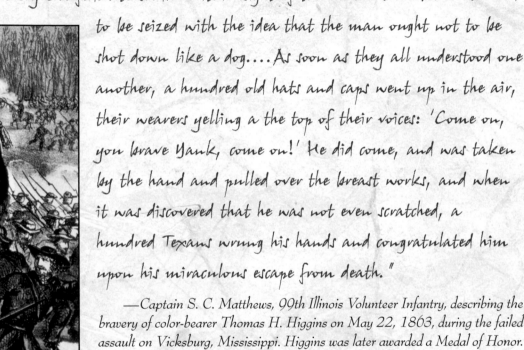

range, but he never faltered. Stumbling over the bodies of his fallen comrades, he continued to advance. Suddenly, as if with one impulse, every Confederate soldier within sight of the Union color bearer seemed to be seized with the idea that the man ought not to be shot down like a dog.... As soon as they all understood one another, a hundred old hats and caps went up in the air, their wearers yelling a the top of their voices: 'Come on, you brave Yank, come on!' He did come, and was taken by the hand and pulled over the breast works, and when it was discovered that he was not even scratched, a hundred Texans wrung his hands and congratulated him upon his miraculous escape from death."

—Captain S. C. Matthews, 99th Illinois Volunteer Infantry, describing the bravery of color-bearer Thomas H. Higgins on May 22, 1863, during the failed assault on Vicksburg, Mississippi. Higgins was later awarded a Medal of Honor.

This Currier & Ives print of a Union charge at the Second Battle of Bull Run shows the precarious position color-bearers assumed while attacking or defending breastworks.

This photograph by Alexander Gardner was taken on 1862, after the battle of Antietam.

Photographer Alexander Gardner captured the devastation of Richmond in this April 1865 image. Scenes such as this were all too common across the South. Most of the war had been fought on Confederate territory, and destruction of homes, factories, railroads, and farms was widespread.

Louis Kurz

A lithographer from Chicago, Louis Kurz produced a print of Abraham Lincoln shortly after the President's assassination. Kurz is best known for the three dozen or so prints that he and his partner, Alexander Allison, introduced to a new generation of Americans in the 1880s and 1890s. Although stylized and ridden with errors, Kurz prints were cheap, readily available, and eagerly purchased by people across America whose only experience with the war was from history books.

Kurz and Allison print of the Battle of Olustee, Florida, on February 20, 1864

Williamsburg

In the spring of 1862, Union General George McClellan launched his Virginia Peninsula campaign with 100,000 soldiers. Confederate General Joseph Johnston, outnumbered more than two to one, began a long retreat toward Richmond. In a sharp rearguard action fought near Williamsburg, McClellan suffered more than 2,000 casualties while the rebel force, commanded by General James Longstreet, lost more than 1,700. This action delayed McClellan's Army of the Potomac for several hours, shielded Johnston's supply train, and ensured the continuation of a strong defense of Richmond.

The Union siege of Petersburg, Virginia, lasted nine-and-a-half months, from June 1864 until April 1865. Both sides dug trenches to reinforce themselves and hold their stalemate. One creative attempt to break the siege was made on July 30. Union troops had dug deep under Confederate lines and planted vast amounts of gunpowder. At 4:45 in the morning, they detonated the explosives and tore apart the enemy line above it. But bumbling federal leaders and stiff rebel resistance caused the attacking federal troops, including a division of black soldiers, to get trapped inside the crater formed by the blast. Forced to advance up the newly formed hill after charging into the hole, virtually the entire assault force was annihilated. In a report on the incident, General Grant wrote, "It was the saddest affair I have witnessed in the war."

Friendly Enemies

During lulls between battles, it was **not uncommon for opponents to greet each other and exchange goods.** After all, they did share a common language and culture as well as the experiences of soldiering. **Tobacco, sugar, coffee, and newspapers were among the popular items traded.** When opposing lines were separated by a river or stream, a favorite practice was to float the goods back and forth aboard little handmade sailboats.

An unknown **number of women served in the ranks of both armies** throughout the war. **Some estimates claim the number to be in the hundreds or possibly more than a thousand.** Since women were not allowed to be soldiers, obviously, those who

Frances Clalin, shown here in the uniform of a cavalry trooper of the Missouri militia as well as in more traditional attire, is just one example of such women warriors.

fought had to do so in disguise and in secret. Most were discovered quickly and banished from the camps, but a few are known to have survived through the war undetected. An accurate number of the women who served can never be known.

Cotton Gin

Although the demand for cotton by Northern textile mill owners grew throughout the later half of the 18th century, the manual resources required for preparing it for processing made it an uneconomical crop for many Southern farmers. After harvest, it had taken a slave as many as ten hours to remove one pound of cotton lint from the sticky seed. Due to a lack of adequate workpower, cotton crops would often decay in the fields.

Eli Whitney, a Northern tutor and amateur inventor, learned of this problem while in Georgia in 1793. Whitney later wrote, "All agreed that if a machine could be invented ... it would be a great thing, both to the Country and the inventor."

Within ten days, Whitney developed the cotton gin, a device that used toothed cylinders to separate the cotton fiber from the seed through wire screens. With the gin, planters could process 300 to 1,000 pounds of cotton per day, and cotton production expanded dramatically throughout the South.

The **locomotive General Haupt** pictured here was named in honor of General Herman Haupt, the head of the system of military railroads. In 1864 and 1865, the Union's 365 engines and **more than 4,000 cars transported more than 5 million tons of supplies.**

Southern Weaponry

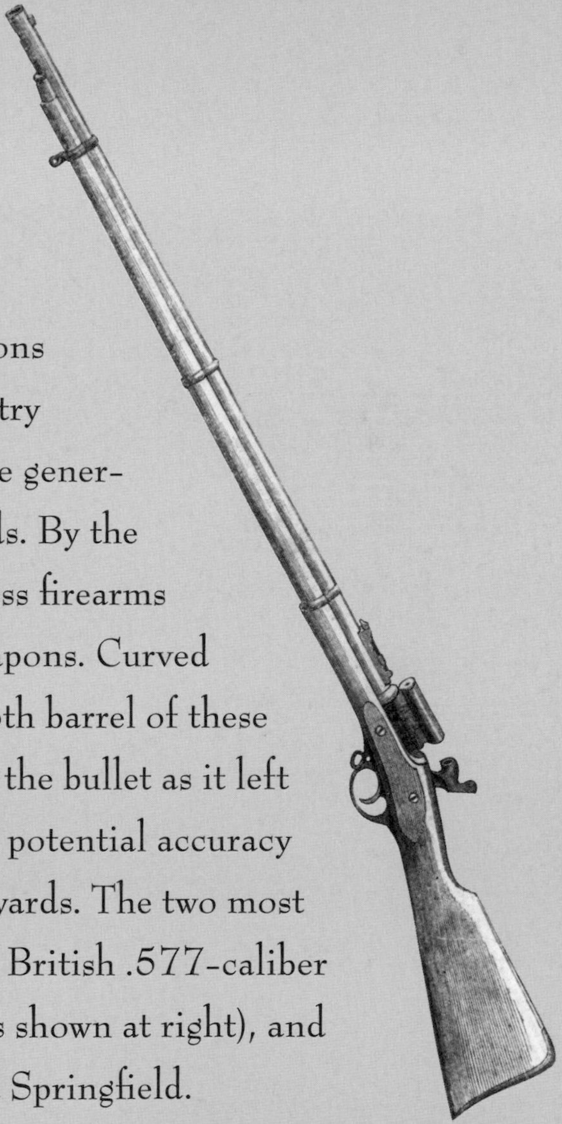

The ancient smoothbore weapons most of the Confederate infantry used at the start of the war were generally ineffective beyond 80 yards. By the middle of 1862, these worthless firearms had been replaced by rifled weapons. Curved grooves were cut into the smooth barrel of these guns to provide a rapid spin to the bullet as it left the barrel, which increased the potential accuracy of the shot to more than 400 yards. The two most popular types of rifles were the British .577-caliber Enfield (a variation of which is shown at right), and the .58-caliber U.S.-produced Springfield.

Fredericksburg

Union General Ambrose Burnside's
130,000-strong Army of the Potomac had
caught the Confederates napping. Forward
elements of his command reached the river
opposite Fredericksburg on November 14,
1862, two days before the rebels. Upset
over the lack of requested pontoon bridges,
however, Burnside decided to wait for their
arrival before crossing. That delay gave
Robert E. Lee's 78,000 troops of the
Army of Northern Virginia time to regain
their footing. When the armies finally
clashed on December 13, Burnside's forces
were unable to break through the securely
entrenched Confederate line. Two nights
after the battle, in the midst of a heavy
rainstorm, Burnside returned his army to
the eastern bank. He suffered about
12,600 casualties to 5,300 for the enemy.

The Wandering Newspaper

Unlike their counterparts throughout the North, **Southern newspapers were constantly under threat of Union occupation as federal troops invaded the South and seized large chunks of territory.** This is one of the reasons that many newspaper titles once published during the Civil War are no longer available for inspection.

One such paper was the *Memphis Appeal*, a paper that had started publication in 1840 and by 1861 was **the largest daily newspaper in Tennessee.** Although it advocated compromise in 1861, the paper's editorial slant became staunchly pro-Confederate after Tennessee left the Union.

The *Appeal's* **press and other equipment left Memphis by rail just before the city was occupied by Union troops in June 1862.** The editors set up shop in Grenada, Mississippi, only to flee again in November when soldiers from Ulysses S. Grant's army moved into that town. The *Appeal* then published in Jackson—Mississippi's state capital—until May 1863, moving next to Atlanta when Grant's troops seized Jackson. In Atlanta, circulation topped 14,000 for the paper's two daily editions. But the *Appeal* had to move again when Sherman captured Atlanta in September 1864. At that time, the paper moved 167 miles to the west to set up in Montgomery, Alabama, where it remained until April 1865, when Yankee troopers from James H. Wilson's cavalry corps seized the city.

The paper's staff continued to elude capture, however, by moving to Columbus, Georgia, where their luck ran out. Many staffers were taken prisoner and some of the equipment wrecked. Editor Benjamin F. Dill was brought before General Wilson. "Have we caught the old fox at last?" exclaimed the general. "Well, I'll be damned." After some laughter and backslapping, the general and editor drank whiskey together. **The press survived and was returned to Memphis, where the paper resumed publication in November. Today, the *Memphis Commercial Appeal* continues the tradition of its earlier name.**

Elizabeth Van Lew, a member of Virginia's aristocracy, had been educated in the North and came to hate slavery. **When the war started, she decided to keep the Lincoln administration informed of events in the Confederate capital.** Using her slaves as couriers, she managed to keep Union authorities up-to-date throughout the entire war and was never suspected of disloyalty to the Confederacy.

Writing in invisible ink with a cipher that she developed, Van Lew was a master of deception. She **managed to get one of her female servants hired as a nanny at the Confederacy's presidential mansion, thus obtaining much valuable information.** She aided escaped prisoners at the same time that she offered her house as quarters for a new commander of Libby Prison. Ruined by war, however, Van Lew was spurned by postwar society. She was appointed postmaster of Richmond by President Ulysses S. Grant but died in poverty.

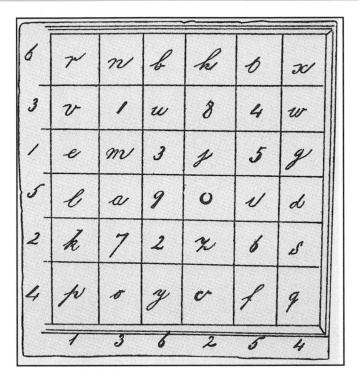

This cipher key was found in Van Lew's effects after her death in 1900. The letters of the alphabet and the numbers *0* through *9* appear in the 6-by-6 grid, which has coordinate numbers at the side and bottom. Using this grid, the letter *m*, for example, would be represented by its coordinates, *13*.

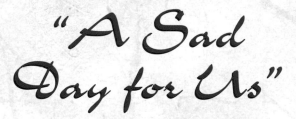

Chapter 6

"A Sad Day for Us"

"This has been a sad day for us,

Colonel—a sad day; but we can't

expect always to gain victories."

—Robert E. Lee, following the devastating failure of
Pickett's Charge at the Battle of Gettysburg

A major question prior to the **1864 presidential election** was how soldiers would be able to vote. **Many states allowed their military troops to cast votes from wherever their units were stationed or from hospitals where they were convalescing.** In states such as Illinois and Connecticut, however, soldiers had to return home to vote. Following the election, **charges of voting irregularities were lodged against the Lincoln administration:** New York Democratic commissioners had been thrown in prison, and only Republicans had visited the regiments in the field. In Ohio camps, there were shortages of Democratic ballots. In the end, **more than 116,000 soldiers voted for Lincoln, with only 33,748 votes going to his Democratic opponent, George B. McClellan,** former commander of the Army of the Potomac.

This engraving, published in Harper's Weekly *on October 29, 1864, is from the sketch "Pennsylvania Soldiers Voting" by William Waud.*

"If the North can march an army right through the South," Union General William T. Sherman wired Ulysses S. Grant in November 1864, "it is proof positive that the North can prevail." Casting free of his supply base in Atlanta, Sherman cut a destructive path through Georgia and South Carolina. He said, "War is cruelty, and you cannot refine it; and those who brought war . . . deserve all the curses and maledictions a people can pour out."

This scene merely hints at the widespread destruction that took place in Columbia, South Carolina, as the city shifted from Confederate to Union control in February 1865.

"All I ask of fate is that I may be killed leading a cavalry charge."

—*Jeb Stuart*

Upon learning that flamboy-
ant cavalry commander
**James Ewell Brown
"Jeb" Stuart** had died
from a mortal wound during
the Battle of Yellow Tavern in Virginia, on May 11, 1864, Robert E. Lee said in
tribute, "He never brought me a piece of false information."

Franklin

By noon on November 30, 1864, Union General John Schofield's 28,000-troop army had fortified trenches around the southern edge of Franklin, Tennessee. With the Harpeth River to his back, he hoped to be able to hold off Confederate General John Hood's 38,000 troops until a bridge could be repaired, allowing his 800-wagon supply train to escape to the north bank. Just as the last of his wagons were almost across the river, Hood's army attacked along a battle line two miles long. During fierce hand-to-hand fighting, Schofield's line held, bolstered by the murderous fire of his artillery. The fight went on until darkness, when more than 6,000 Confederate casualties littered the Tennessee countryside, including the bodies of six generals killed or mortally wounded during the failed attack. Union losses were about 2,300. Two hours after the fighting ended, the Union army abandoned Franklin and marched toward Nashville.

The estate of Arlington in Virginia, across the Potomac River from Washington, D.C., was the family home of Martha Washington's grandson, George Washington Parke Custis. Custis's daughter, **Mary Anna,** married **Robert E. Lee,** and the Lees **made Arlington their home.** With the **outbreak of war,** Union General Irvin McDowell crossed the river and occupied

the area, using the mansion as his headquarters. **The Lees relocated their residence to Richmond.**

Union dead began to be buried at the Arlington estate in June 1864. General Montgomery C. Meigs wanted soldiers **buried as close to the mansion as possible to discourage Robert E. Lee or his family from ever returning to live there.** The site ultimately **became Arlington National Cemetery.** Arlington House, the home of the Custises and the Lees, continues to look over the grave sites of some of America's heroes.

Pauline Cushman

One of the more flam-boyant spies during the war was Pauline Cushman, reputed to have been the subject of the later silent movie series, *The Perils of Pauline.* Cushman, born in New Orleans but raised in Michigan, was an aspiring actress whose soldier husband died of dysentery in 1862. Recruited into espionage service for the

Union, Cushman, during a play in Louisville in early 1863, drank a toast to the Confederacy and was subsequently fired from the cast. Her supposed Southern sympathies now established, she moved south to Union-occupied Nashville but was expelled for her Southern leanings.

Cushman was acting on a military order to learn what she could about Confederate General Braxton Bragg's plans. Suspicion fell upon her and she was **arrested, with sensitive drawings and plans found on her person. A court-martial examined her case and sentenced her to death by hanging.** Before this sentence could be carried out, however, Union troops advanced and occupied Shelbyville, Tennessee, where Cushman was confined to a sickbed. Rescued, she went on to tour the North, lecturing on her exploits and garnering accolades wherever she went. Her career went ever downward, however, and she died in 1893 from an intentional overdose of opium.

The Wilderness

General Ulysses S. Grant, recently named General in Chief of all Union armies, led more than 120,000 troops into an area of Virginia called the Wilderness on May 5, 1864. His plan was to pass around the right flank of the 66,000-strong Confederate Army of Northern Virginia to place Union troops between the rebels and Richmond. While the Union troops were marching in columns along narrow roads through dense forest, General Robert E. Lee's army struck, neutralizing Grant's numerical advantage. Two days later, some 17,600 Union and more than 7,500 Confederate troops were casualties, many succumbing to one of a number of brush fires consuming parts of the Wilderness. This was the first action in an 11-month campaign that would ultimately end with Lee's surrender.

Spotsylvania Court House

After the fighting in the Virginia Wilderness ended, Grant turned his army, now numbering 100,000, to the southeast in an attempt to out-flank Lee. Once he discovered Grant's intention, Lee raced his 50,000 soldiers ahead of the Union army, beating it to the outskirts of Spotsylvania Court House. From May 8 to May 18, 1864, a series of Union assaults failed to drive the rebels from their defenses. Finally, after nearly 17,500 Union and 10,000 Confederate casualties, Grant withdrew to make another attempt to outflank Lee in this bloody war of attrition.

The CSS *Sumter* frequently escaped past the Union blockade into the Gulf of Mexico during the first year of the war.
Commanded by Raphael Semmes, who was instructed "to do

the enemy's commerce the greatest injury in the shortest time," the *Sumter* captured or destroyed 18 Union vessels in six months. Mechanical trouble forced its sale to a British buyer in January 1862.

This is how the field officers and staff broke down in a regulation regiment:

Field and Staff	# of men with this rank
Colonel	1
Lieutenant Colonel	1
Major	1
Adjutant	1
Quartermaster	1
Surgeon (Rank of Major)	1
Asst. Surgeons	2
Chaplain	1
Sergeant-Major	1
Quartermaster's Sergeant	1
Commissary-Sergeant	1
Hospital Steward	1
Principal Musicians	2

According to regulations, a regiment consisted of ten companies (the breakdown of each company is shown at right), but these regimental positions belonged to no company.

Theoretically, a regiment consisted of 1,025 troops, however very few regiments

Company Formation	# of men with this rank
Captain	1
First Lieutenant	1
Second Lieutenant	1
First Sergeant	1
Sergeants	4
Corporals	8
Musicians	2
Wagoner	1
Privates	82

approached that figure after several months in the field. It was not unusual later in the war for a Union or Confederate regiment to number no greater than 200. The Union's practice was to raise new regiments rather than reinforce those already in the field, while Confederates typically filled open slots in established regiments. That's why a rough total of 2,100 regiments served in the Union army by the end of the war, while Confederates fielded only about 680.

Medical Discoveries

Southern doctors made important accidental discoveries during the war. One incident occurred at Chattanooga, Tennessee, when surgeons ran out of chloroform, which was used to kill maggots that infested many wounds. The doctors were amazed when maggot-infested wounds healed more quickly than clean wounds because the insects acted as scavengers, eating the diseased tissue. This "cure" had been known in medieval times but had been forgotten by 1861.

A Confederate field hospital following the August 1862 battle at Cedar Mountain, Virginia.

Civil War Challenge

Battle of Spotsylvania Court House

1. What Union general was killed by Confederate snipers seconds after his remark that the enemy could not hit an elephant at that distance?
2. For how many days did the fight around Spotsylvania Court House take place?
3. On May 12, in the pouring rain, Ulysses S. Grant's troops attacked a heavily defended position shaped like a half circle. What was the nickname given to this location?
4. What is the second nickname given to this position by veterans of the battle?
5. Name the battle that immediately preceded the Battle of Spotsylvania Court House.

Civil War Challenge Answers

1. General John Sedgwick
2. 10 days
3. The Mule Shoe
4. Bloody Angle
5. The Battle of the Wilderness

250 THE CIVIL WAR

"A private soldier's world does not extend far beyond... his immediate vicinity of action. Imagine... then how eagerly he longed for the arrival of the newspapers."

—Edwin Forbes, prolific artist/correspondent for Frank Leslie's Illustrated Newspaper

The "Dictator" was a 13-inch mortar that weighed more than 17,000 pounds and could hurl a 220-pound ball more than two miles. This iron monster was transported via railroad to Union siege lines around Petersburg, Virginia, to bombard the Confederate defenses.

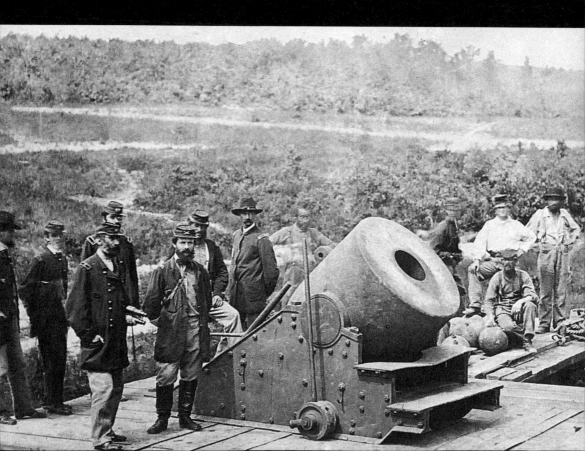

A string of field obstructions are shown protecting a Confederate sand-bagged redoubt near the Potter homestead outside of Atlanta, Georgia. Chevaux-de-frise (spiked timber) and palisades (wooden slats driven into the ground) were constructed along this line. Some of the wood came from the stripped outbuildings that can be seen near the fortifications.

Mary Todd Lincoln

"No lady of the White House has ever been so maltreated by the public press," wrote the editor of the *Chicago Daily Tribune* in August 1861. Throughout the war, Mary Todd Lincoln was constantly attacked by the press, and her personality foibles made such attacks easy.

Kentucky-born, Mary Todd married Abraham Lincoln in 1842. Strong-willed and tempestuous with a sharp tongue, she was also undisciplined, a spendthrift with lavish tastes, and emotionally immature. But Lincoln loved her dearly and defended her time after time.

Mary fussed constantly over Lincoln's appointments, and her imperious manner made her many enemies. Because four of her brothers and two brothers-in-law served in the Confederate army, she was constantly accused of spying for the enemy. In addition to her political troubles, the 1862 death of the Lincolns' 12-year-old son Willie devastated her.

Her husband's assassination so grieved Mary that she took no part in the funeral ceremonies. She finally left the White House a month later. Her son Robert caused his mother to stand trial for insanity in 1875. After being institutionalized for a few months, she was released and went to Europe, returning to America in 1880. Mary Todd Lincoln died lonely and isolated. Her autopsy revealed a brain tumor that may have played a large part in her character.

This photograph of a Federal picket post was taken shortly before the Battle of Atlanta.

Civil War Challenge
Battle of Atlanta

1. Why did the Army of Tennessee fight the Army of the Tennessee?
2. On what date did Union troops arrive at the outskirts of Atlanta?
3. On what date did Union troops enter the city following Hood's evacuation of Atlanta?
4. What Union commander of the Army of the Tennessee was killed outside Atlanta on July 22, 1864?
5. The capture of what city in Georgia by Union troops caused Hood to evacuate Atlanta?

Civil War Challenge Answers

1. The Union often named its armies after rivers, so the Union Army of the Tennessee was named after the Tennessee River. The Confederacy named its armies after geographic areas, so the rebel Army of Tennessee was named after the state of Tennessee. These two armies happened to meet in Atlanta, Georgia.
2. July 17, 1864
3. September 2, 1864
4. Union General James McPherson
5. Jonesboro, Georgia

Lincoln visited officers of the Army of the Potomac on October 3, 1862, at the battlefield **at Antietam after their victory.** General George McClellan is shown facing Lincoln on the left. Captain George Custer, who in 1876 would be killed at Little Big Horn by the Sioux, is at the far right.

Soldiers whiled away the off-hours when they were stuck in camp by trying to keep busy. Some of the troops created intriguing works of art. One soldier painted this spoon to show a man standing guard over the camp. Others would whittle on whatever pieces of wood or bone they could find. The bone trinkets shown here are a lapel pin and two tie clasps. Private William A. Failor, Company G, 202nd Pennsylvania, produced the clasp on the left.

The New York *Herald* was the only Northern newspaper to organize its correspondents who covered military operations. While other reporters eked out an existence dependent upon the goodwill of officers, the *Herald* provided tents, supplies, and forage for its employees.

"None on that crest now need be told that the enemy is advancing. Every eye could see his legions, an overwhelming resistless tide of an ocean of armed men sweeping upon us! Regiment after regiment and brigade after brigade move from the woods and rapidly take their places in the lines forming the assault. . . . More than half a mile their front extends; more than a thousand yards the dull gray masses deploy, man touching man, rank pressing rank, and line supporting line. The red flags wave, their horsemen gallop up and down; the arms of eighteen thousand men, barrel and bayonet, gleam in the sun, a sloping forest of flashing steel. Right on they move, as with one soul, in perfect order, without impediment of ditch, or wall or stream, over ridge and slope through orchard and meadows, and cornfield, magnificent, grim, irresistible."

—Union Lieutenant Frank A. Haskell, on Pickett's Charge

Union soldiers enjoy a bath during a lull in the fighting after the battles around Spotsylvania Court House, Virginia. During active campaigns, soldiers had little opportunity for personal hygiene. "Some of the men were just as particular about changing their underclothing at least once a week as they would be at home," recalled a veteran, "while others would do so only under the severest pressure."

Civil War Challenge

Match the ship with its primary battle or the port where it sunk:

Ship	Battle
USS *Kearsarge*	Mobile Bay
CSS *Yazoo*	Cherbourg, France
USS *Tecumseh*	Charleston
CSS *Hunley*	Cherbourg, France
USS *Minnesota*	Mobile Bay
CSS *Alabama*	Island #10
USS *Cairo*	Hampton Roads
CSS *Albemarle*	Charleston
USS *Housatonic*	Vicksburg
CSS *Tennessee*	Plymouth

Civil War Challenge
Answers

Ship	Battle	Ship	Battle
USS *Kearsarge*	Cherbourg, France	CSS *Alabama*	Cherbourg, France
CSS *Yazoo*	Island #10	USS *Cairo*	Vicksburg
USS *Tecumseh*	Mobile Bay	CSS *Albemarle*	Plymouth
CSS *Hunley*	Charleston	USS *Housatonic*	Charleston
USS *Minnesota*	Hampton Roads	CSS *Tennessee*	Mobile Bay

Photography was barely 30 years old at the time of the Civil War, but technical advances meant that photos were inexpensive and readily available for soldiers to record their participation in the war. These soldiers display a variety of uniforms. The drum at top left may have been official issue, but the guitar below it most defi-nitely was not. The careful precision of these uniforms disappeared soon after the war began. Shortages of all kinds plagued both sides and affected what soldiers wore.

This midnight scene depicts the March 14, 1863, **attempt by seven Union ships to run past the earthworks forts at Port Hudson,** about 25 miles upriver from Baton Rouge, Louisiana. By the time the USS *Mississippi* was sunk, the other ship captains were losing their will to continue. They saw the work done by the **Confederate gunners on the heavy British-imported Armstrong cannon,** which could throw 135-pound shells. The naval repulse resulted in a retreat by the Union army.

Wilson's Creek

Union General Nathaniel Lyon launched a surprise attack with 5,500 against a Confederate force twice that number at Wilson's Creek, Missouri, on August 10, 1861. The rebel force commanded by General Ben McCulloch formed a solid formation, three and four ranks deep, amid scrub oak on a rock-ribbed slope. The "lines would approach again and again within less than fifty yards of each other," wrote a Confederate officer, "and then after delivering a deadly fire, each would fall back ... reform and reload, only to advance again." Each side suffered about 1,300 casualties before the Union troops were driven from the field. While attempting to lead a desperate countercharge, Lyon was hit by a bullet that punctured his chest and knocked him to the ground. He died moments later.

Chapter 7

"In Great Deeds Something Abides"

Ulysses S. Grant leads his troops in an assault on Confederate fortifications at Vicksburg, Mississippi.

"In great deeds something abides. On great fields something stays. Forms change and pass; bodies disappear, but spirits linger, to consecrate ground for the vision-place of souls. And reverent men and women from afar, and generations that know us  not and that we know not of, heart-drawn to see where and by whom great things were suffered and done for them, shall come to this deathless field to ponder and dream; And lo! the shadow of a mighty presence shall wrap them in its bosom, and the power of the vision pass into their souls."

—Joshua Chamberlain, heroic commander of the 20th Maine during the Battle of Gettysburg, in a speech at the battlefield on October 3, 1889

If the adage that "an army travels on its stomach" is true, then the armies of the blue and gray covered a good bit of the distance on **hardtack.** Otherwise called crackers, army bread, or hard bread, hardtack was **a staple food of soldiers during the war.** A simple flour-and-water biscuit, hardtack **measured approximately three inches by three inches and was half an inch thick. It was often eaten plain—or crumbled, boiled, or fried.** "Hardtack was not so bad an article of food, even when traversed by insects," recalled one veteran. "Eaten in the dark, no one could tell the difference between it and hardtack that was untenanted."

Nashville

In December 1864, Union General George Thomas's army around Nashville, Tennessee, was growing. General John Schofield's 25,000 troops had joined after their victory at Franklin, bringing the number under Thomas's command to almost 80,000. Once Confederate General John Hood's Army of Tennessee reached the southern edge of town, it occupied itself by fortifying earthworks. Hood knew his poorly equipped and underfed force of less than 30,000 was no match for Thomas, especially after its devastating defeat at Franklin.

After much prodding by Ulysses S. Grant, Thomas finally left his defenses and struck the rebels on December 15. Hood's meager line gave way under the weight of Thomas's attack, and the Confederates retreated to a last-ditch line on a low range of hills two miles south of their original position. When Union troops renewed the fight the next afternoon, the rebels began to fall back. The retreat quickly degenerated into a rout, ending any form of organized resistance. Thomas lost about 3,000 over the two days of fighting. While reports failed to mention the number of Hood's casualties, almost 4,000 soldiers were listed as captured. An entire Confederate army practically ceased to exist as a fighting unit after the battle. The war in the West was nearly at an end.

Robert Smalls was a slave living in South Carolina. Before the war, his master had allowed him to hire himself out to others, so Smalls had accumulated a variety of skills. Working as a sailor on the *Planter,* a cotton steamer in Charleston, Smalls came under control of the Confederate government when it chartered the vessel after war broke out. Smalls's skills were recognized by his superiors, and he became the de facto pilot of the ship, although his status as a slave kept him from officially gaining that title. Along with that position came considerable knowledge of the signals and pass codes necessary for a vessel to navigate around the heavily fortified harbor.

On the night of May 12, 1862, the captain of the *Planter* and his entire white crew went ashore, leaving the steamer in the hands of Smalls and the seven other black crewhands. Early the next morning, Smalls commandeered the ship, picked up his family and some other slaves seeking freedom, and set sail for the Union fleet blockading Charleston Harbor. Sailing waters with which he was well familiar, Smalls navigated through the Confederate armaments with the appropriate pass codes and approached the USS *Onward*. The black sailors realized they were on an enemy vessel, so they flew a white sheet of surrender to prevent the Union navy from firing on them. **Smalls's escape to freedom was a sensation around the world.** He personally

lobbied President Lincoln and Secretary of War Edwin Stanton to establish regiments of black soldiers. He **served with distinction in the Union forces** throughout the rest of the war and returned to South Carolina during Reconstruction, where he **entered politics and ultimately won election to the U.S. House of Representatives.**

This engraving of the Battle of Shiloh is based upon a painting by Alonzo Chappel.

Civil War Challenge
Battle of Shiloh

1. What were the dates of the battle?
2. What name did veterans of the battle give to the impenetrable oak thicket that was the center of heavy fighting on the first day?
3. Name the church that played a prominent role in the battle.
4. By the end of the first day, Ulysses S. Grant's Union troops were pushed back to the outskirts of a small town resting on the Tennessee River. Name the town.
5. General Lew Wallace's division reinforced Grant's beleaguered command the night of the first day. Wallace is better known as an author than as a Union general. What book did he write?

Civil War Challenge Answers

1. April 6 and April 7, 1862
2. The Hornet's Nest
3. Shiloh Church
4. Pittsburg Landing
5. *Ben Hur*

The New State of West Virginia

The state of Virginia was as divided over the issues of the Civil War as was the nation itself. Citizens of the mountainous counties in western Virginia were more pro-Union than pro-Confederate. The Allegheny and Blue Ridge mountains cut westerners off from other Virginians, and rivers such as the Monongahela, the Kanawha, and the Ohio put them in close contact with Northerners in Pennsylvania and Ohio. For some time westerners had viewed the state government as representing Tidewater-area plantation owners with no interest in them.

After voting against Virginia secession in 1861, it was only a matter of time before the western counties organized themselves to leave the state. Early Union victories in the area provided them with military backing.

The U.S. Constitution declares, "No new states shall be formed or erected within the jurisdiction of any other state … without the consent of the legislatures of the states concerned." But Virginia's secession from the Union left a vacuum western Virginians were only too happy to fill. In Wheeling, delegates from the western counties declared themselves the Restored Government of Virginia and voted themselves out of the state. Congress agreed to admit the new state, and in June 1863 West Virginia was welcomed into the Union.

Names for the Conflict

Though widely known today as the Civil War, this conflict has had many other names. When the government began publishing *The Official Records* in the 1880s, bringing together reports, orders, and correspondence from both sides of the conflict, it used the name "War of the Rebellion" to denote the event. Later, the name "War Between the States" crept into public usage, generally as a result of Southern hatred of the term *rebellion*. To many in the South, the war was—and still is—"The War of Northern Aggression" or "The War for Southern Independence." Some Yankees have called it "The War for the Preservation of the Union" or "The War of Secession." Others have avoided the term *war* altogether, using euphemisms such as "The Late Unpleasantness." In the 20th century, the federal government settled on the generic name "Civil War" as the generally accepted title for the conflict.

Perhaps the most infamous intelligence network used by federal troops during the war was that of **Allan Pinkerton**. Before the war, Pinkerton had **founded a detective agency that continues as a security firm today.** In 1861, he uncovered and foiled an assassination plot against President-elect Lincoln. Having won Lincoln's confidence, Pinkerton joined the staff of an old friend, General George McClellan, to coordinate intelligence-gathering activities. **His espionage organization ran spies behind Confederate lines.**

Thomas J. "Stonewall" Jackson

"This is no ordinary war. The brave and gallant Federal officers are the very kind that must be killed. Shoot the brave officers and the cowards will run away and take the men with them." Such was Stonewall Jackson's response to a report that one of his subordinates had attempted to save the life of a brave Union officer during the heat of battle. Jackson felt that this war was far different from the chivalrous conflicts of earlier times. He recognized the importance of never giving the enemy a second chance.

Jackson's commitment to total victory often extended to the treatment of his own troops. To a request from one of his officers to visit his dying wife, Jackson replied, "Man, man, do you love your wife more than your country?" When the colonel of one of his regiments objected to an attack on the grounds that his "regiment would be exterminated," Jackson responded, "Colonel, do your duty. I have made every arrangement to care for the wounded and bury the dead."

While his actions and decisions embittered some officers and enlisted soldiers, most followed him with a devotion unmatched during the course of the war. Jackson led by example, and his victories made those who followed him proud to belong to his command.

Jackson was born on January 21, 1824, in Clarksburg, Virginia. He graduated from West Point in 1846 and served in the Mexican War. Having resigned his commission in 1852, he became a professor of artillery and natural philosophy at the Virginia Military Institute (VMI).

At VMI, Jackson earned a reputation for eccentricity that carried over to the war. His extreme religious beliefs, nonmilitary manner of dress, strange dietary habits (such as eating lemons during battle), and reluctance to fight on Sunday are just a few of the quirks that added to his mystique.

From the First Battle of Bull Run until his death at Chancellorsville, Jackson's presence on a battlefield was a significant factor in the Confederates' favor.

On Friday, October 2, 1862, Alexander Gardner photographed the President in front of this tent near the Antietam battlefield. On the left of the photo is Allan Pinkerton, the famous detective, with General John M. McClernand on the right.

Popular Books on the Civil War

The American Heritage New History of the Civil War
  by Bruce Catton and James McPherson

Battle Cry of Freedom: The Civil War Era
  by James McPherson

The Civil War: A Narrative (3 volumes)
  by Shelby Foote

Glory Road
  by Bruce Catton

Gods and Generals
by Jeff Shaara

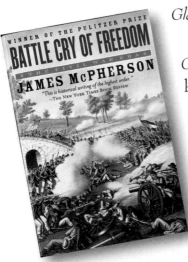

Gone With the Wind by Margaret Mitchell

The Killer Angels by Michael Shaara

Mr. Lincoln's Army by Bruce Catton

A Stillness at Appomattox by Bruce Catton

*This Hallowed Ground: The Story of the Union Side
of the Civil War* by Bruce Catton

As the siege of Petersburg dragged on through 1864 and into 1865, officers and enlisted troops alike burrowed into the ground for protection from enemy artillery and sniper fire. Soldiers in both armies constructed a variety of ingenious shelters, making use of whatever material was at hand. This is the interior of a Confederate fortification.

Alfred Waud

The war's preeminent special artist was English-born Alfred Waud. He had 344 sketches published by *Harper's Weekly* and the New York *Illustrated News*. A fellow member of the press described him as "blue-eyed, fairbearded, strapping and stalwart, full of loud cheery laughs and comic songs, armed to the teeth, jack-booted, gauntleted, slouch-hatted, yet clad in the shooting-jacket of a civilian." The list of engagements at which he was present included most of the major battles in the Eastern Theater: both battles of Bull Run, Burnside's North Carolina expedition, the Peninsula Campaign, Antietam, Fredericksburg, Chancellorsville, Gettysburg, the Wilderness, Cold Harbor, the Shenandoah Valley Campaign, Petersburg, and Appomattox. His brother William was also a sketch artist during the war.

This picture of an ambulance wagon was taken at the Battle of Bull Run.

How a Typical Photograph Was Taken

The photographer first selected a glass plate, usually 8 by 10 inches for wider views or 4 by 10 inches for the popular stereo images. The plate was coated with collodion made of a solution of nitrocellulose in equal parts of sulphuric ether and 95-proof alcohol. The surface of the plate was then sensitized by adding bromide and iodine of potassium or ammonia. After allowing this mixture to evaporate to the right consistency, the plate was immersed for three to five minutes in a bath holder solution of silver nitrate. This had to be done in total darkness, or in amber light at most. The plate next went into a holder to protect it from light, and the plate and holder were then inserted into the camera, already aimed and focused. The photographer uncapped the lens to permit an exposure of five to thirty seconds, depending on available light. Following the capping of the lens, the photographer had only a few minutes to develop the plate in a solution of sulfate of iron and acetic acid. Finally, the plate was washed with a cyanide of potassium solution to remove any surplus silver before it was washed, dried, and varnished.

More than 2,300 chaplains served in the Union army throughout the war. Sixty-six died in service, and three were given the Medal of Honor. In this photo, **Father Thomas Mooney celebrates Catholic mass for members of the 69th New York Infantry.** The regiment's commander, Colonel Michael Corcoran, stands to the left of the priest.

To help supplement drab army rations, the government appointed **civilian vendors, or sutlers,** to sell a wide variety of goods in camp. Unscrupulous sutlers **often jacked up the prices and took unfair advantage of troops.** Many of these profiteers became the target of pranks and vandalism from disgruntled soldiers.

Sally Tompkins

The only woman to hold a military commission in the Confederate army was Sally Tompkins. Virginian by birth, she came from a wealthy family that moved to Richmond prior to the beginning of hostilities. When wounded soldiers began arriving, casualties of the First Battle of Bull Run, **Tompkins established a hospital in the donated home of Judge John Robertson.** She attracted other well-bred ladies, who brought their personal and monetary aid to the new Robertson Hospital. **"The little lady with the milk-white hands,"** as she was known, carried on in spite of her frail appearance. Later in 1861 when the Confederate government took over control of all hospitals, **President Jefferson Davis commissioned Tompkins as a captain so she could continue administering to the sick and wounded.** Between August 1861 and June 1865, Robertson Hospital received 1,333 admissions and numerous transfers with only 73 deaths—a remarkable record for the time.

Confederate prisoners wait to be transported north from Chattanooga, Tennessee, in 1864. Prison populations overflowed on both sides once Union General Ulysses S. Grant suspended prisoner exchange in April 1864. "Every man we hold," Grant wrote, "when released on parole or otherwise, becomes an active soldier against us. . . . If a system of exchange liberates all prisoners taken, we will have to fight on until the whole South is exterminated."

Vicksburg

General Grant spent seven months of frustrating and tough campaigning before his 75,000-strong Army of the Tennessee was close enough to place Vicksburg, Mississippi, under siege. He met stiff resistance from the citizens of the town and the 30,000-strong Confederate army of General John Pemberton. For 48 days the rebels held out, fighting hunger, disease, and mounting Union pressure. One young housewife later wrote of rats "hanging dressed in the market" and of a friend who had eaten one to find its flavor "fully equal to that of squirrels." Dogs and cats were also noticeably absent from city streets.

With no prospects of reinforcements and his own army too weak to attempt a breakout, Pemberton requested terms of surrender. Grant demanded unconditional surrender, which the Confederate commander promptly refused. They finally agreed on more liberal terms, which included the parole of 30,000 rebel troops. Vicksburg officially surrendered on July 4, 1863, day 48 of the siege and the day after the end of the Battle of Gettysburg. With Vicksburg in Union hands, other smaller rebel garrisons surrendered or were abandoned, opening the Mississippi River to Union shipping and effectively splitting the Confederacy in two.

Vicksburg National Military Park

The Vicksburg National Cemetery was created by the War Department in 1866. It holds about 17,000 Union dead. Congress authorized the creation of the Vicksburg National Military Park on February 18, 1899, and named a commission of three to oversee its development. One of the three was Confederate General Stephen D. Lee, who had commanded a rebel brigade during the Union siege. As with many of the other national military parks, Vicksburg passed to the National Park Service in 1933. Unique to the park is the presence of the remains of the USS *Cairo*, which had sunk in the Yazoo River a year before the city fell into Union hands. More than 1,300 markers and monuments were erected and dedicated by veterans across the park's 1,732 acres.

"The figures on the right are coming in with the new clothing, in the Centre pitching the old rags overboard, & going out on the left to get their rations."

—*William Waud describes the scene in his 1864 sketch of returning prisoners of war*

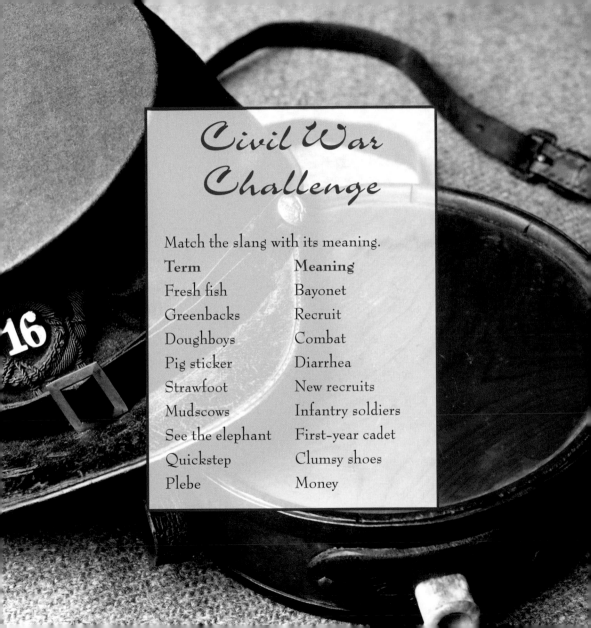

Civil War Challenge

Match the slang with its meaning.

Term	Meaning
Fresh fish	Bayonet
Greenbacks	Recruit
Doughboys	Combat
Pig sticker	Diarrhea
Strawfoot	New recruits
Mudscows	Infantry soldiers
See the elephant	First-year cadet
Quickstep	Clumsy shoes
Plebe	Money

Civil War Challenge Answers

Term	Meaning
Fresh fish	New recruits
Greenbacks	Money
Doughboys	Infantry soldiers
Pig sticker	Bayonet
Strawfoot	Recruit
Mudscows	Clumsy shoes
See the elephant	Combat
Quickstep	Diarrhea
Plebe	First-year cadet

Sharpshooters filled an important role in both the Northern and Southern armies. The Union organized regiments of these skilled soldiers under Colonel Hiram Berdan, who had developed his own methods of training for shooting accuracy and proficiency. The Confederates followed suit and established similar elite units of their own. **Sharpshooters were often the first to scout and secure an area in advance of an army. They were also the last to leave, providing cover for the army's retreat.**

A small steamer, mounting a torpedo at the end of its spar, chugged up the Roanoke River in the darkness of October 27, 1864. Lieutenant William Cushing led 14 troops on a volunteer mission to sink the Confederate ironclad CSS *Albemarle* near Plymouth, North Carolina. Spotted by the enemy before they could reach the craft, they pushed forward under fire. As his craft approached the rebel ship, Cushing discovered that the ship was surrounded by logs to stop any attempt to place a torpedo near it. Gaining speed, his steamer successfully crossed over the barrier. While still under heavy fire, Cushing coolly maneuvered the torpedo against the *Albemarle's* hull. He then pulled a lanyard that set off an explosion and sank the enemy vessel. Unable to cross back over the log barrier, Cushing and his troops were forced to abandon ship. Of the 15 who set off on the mission, 2 drowned, 11 were captured and 2, including Cushing, made a successful escape. Without the rebel ironclad to defend it, Plymouth fell to the Union navy. Cushing earned a promotion to lieutenant commander and received the thanks of Congress.

Standing at the center of this photograph is Admiral David D. Porter, commander of the North Atlantic Blockading Squadron, aboard his flagship, the USS Malvern, *in December 1864. William Cushing stands at far left.*

On November 24, 1863, General Joseph Hooker's 10,000 federal troops stormed the summit of Lookout Mountain, Tennessee, in an engagement that was part of the Battle of Chattanooga. They took the position from 7,000 of Braxton Bragg's soldiers perched atop the peak. In years to come, it would be popularized as the "Battle Above the Clouds" because of the patches of fog that shrouded areas of Lookout Mountain's slopes.

> *"War means fighting, and fighting means killing."*
>
> —*Nathan Bedford Forrest*

A successful business professional at the start of the war, **Nathan Bedford Forrest** joined the Confederate army and quickly advanced to the rank of major general. He was **known for his strategic strikes against Union supply lines and strongholds.** After the war, one of his antagonists, General William Sherman, said he believed Forrest to be "the most remarkable man our Civil War produced on either side." Forrest **was later integral in the formation of the Ku Klux Klan.**

Soldiers on both sides quickly learned to live off the land, particularly when they were in enemy territory. This picture depicts Confederate troops ransacking in New Windsor, Maryland, but the most notorious foraging probably took place along Sherman's March through Georgia. Supply lines for the 60,000 federal troops in that campaign had to be cut loose, so specific units were assigned to find food for the troops. These "bummers" would sometimes return with legitimate forage, but other times their spoils would be the result of looting houses and stores they encountered along the way.

On April 14, 1865, five days after Robert E. Lee's surrender, President Abraham Lincoln was shot by John Wilkes Booth at Ford's Theatre in Washington while watching the comedy *Our American Cousin*. Lincoln died at 7:22 A.M. the next day. After an extensive manhunt, Booth was cornered and killed in Virginia on April 26.

President and Mrs. Lincoln sat in the box on the right as they watched the play at Ford's Theatre. John Wilkes Booth stepped up behind the President, placed a derringer pistol less than six inches from the back of Lincoln's head, and pulled the trigger.

Index